$25.00

D0161258

The American Small Town

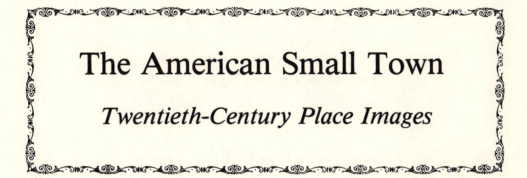

The American Small Town

Twentieth-Century Place Images

John A. Jakle

Archon Books

1982

First published 1982 as an Archon Book,
an imprint of The Shoe String Press, Inc.,
Hamden, Connecticut 06514

Printed in the United States of America

Library of Congress Cataloging in Publication Data

Jakle, John A.
The American small town.

Bibliography: p.
Includes index.
1. United States—Social life and customs—20th century.
2. City and town life—United States. 3. United States—
Popular culture. I. Title.
El69.J24   973.9   81-8090
ISBN 0-208-01919-7   AACR2

For Aberdeen and Abilene.
For Academia, Accotink, and Acmetonia.
For Alabaster, Albion, and Altamont.
For American Fork.
Apache Junction, Apalachicola, Appomattox.
Arab, Arbuckle, Arp.
Arroyo Seco.
Auburn, Aurora, Auxvasse.
And for all the other American small towns.

Contents

Preface

This book was conceived as a collection of photographs descriptive of American small-town landscapes in the early twentieth century. Early in my research it became evident that photographs said as much about the images of place as they did about the realities of place—that photographs could be used as a source of information about small-town stereotypes. (Unless otherwise indicated, the illustrations are from my own collection.) I broadened my research to embrace other sources descriptive of small-town images. Especially useful were novels in which plot and characters grew out of fictionalized small-town settings, and case studies descriptive of small-town life written by social scientists. From my various sources I describe in essay form the stereotypes which Americans assigned to small towns as places. Early chapters concern the images of commerce, life-style, life cycle, and community widely shared at the height of the railroad period when small towns were more self-contained and inward-focused as places. Later chapters concern the impact of the automobile, and the changes which increased geographical mobility brought both to small-town landscapes and to the idea of the small town as a place type.

I am concerned with the American small town as an idealized place. Americans have traditionally considered small towns to be different from cities. Although many small towns serve agriculture, Americans have traditionally differentiated town life from farm life. The small town stands between the farm and the city with its own spectrum of social values. It is not my intention to picture the typical American town; there is no such place, as every town is different according to its region, its time of origin and growth, and its changing economy, among other measures. It is not my intention to write a history of small-town America, for small-town history is necessarily local history given the peculiarities of time, place, and function. I am concerned to describe the idea of the typical American town—to identify the prevailing social stereotypes which Americans used to picture the small town as a distinctive kind of place, and to describe the elements of landscape which traditionally served to symbolize that place type.

The information available to the student of small-town images is immense. Newspapers, magazines, motion pictures, and, indeed, any and every record of American popular culture is potentially a source of understanding. Unfortunately, very little of this information has been distilled from its raw form. My heavy reliance on novelists and their view of the small town overcomes this shortcoming in part. Novelists were forced to distill the varied images of small towns in creating settings for their novels. As novelists dealt in stereotypes, their works remain a vital source for understanding stereotypes. Authors like Sinclair Lewis profoundly influenced American thought about small towns. Novels, like Lewis's *Main Street*, not only reflected stereotypes, but helped create them. Most Americans in the early twentieth century visualized townscapes in photographic terms. Since photographers also pictured small towns in stereotyped ways, photographs represent another valuable source for understanding stereotypes. Social scientists also sought to generalize about small-town society in case studies and other works, and in so doing both reflected and created stereotypes in their own way.

I have set limitations on my work. First, I emphasize the period 1900 to 1960 in order to treat small towns at the height of the railroad era, and to assess the initial impact of the automobile on changing small-town social values and landscapes. Second, I focus on modest-sized places of some economic and social diversity, generally ignoring the smallest hamlets and villages which were rooted exclusively in agriculture, mining, or some other single activity. I also tend to slight the more diversified industrial towns which functioned more as small cities. I emphasize towns with a population of between five hundred and ten thousand. Although this population range had different implications for the character of American town life from decade to decade, it will give the reader a rule of thumb for judging the kind of place I view the American small town to have been.

My view of the small town has a decided Midwestern bias. This view derives not only from my own background as a Midwesterner, but from the realization that Midwestern towns—characterized by ''Main Street'' and other landscape accouterments—did, indeed, symbolize towns nationwide. The most widely publicized small-town novels of the period were those with Midwestern settings. Likewise, the more geographical of the sociological case studies were also researched in the Midwest—such works as *Plainville* by James West, and *Plainville Fifteen Years Later* by Art Gallaher. The bulk of the small-town photography available in archives also seems to have a Midwestern bias. Commercial photographers were more numerous in the towns of the Midwest and seem to have focused more on town themes. In other sections of the country, wilderness, rural, and metropolitan orientations seem to have prevailed. Donald Meinig has proposed ''Main Street of Middle America'' as one of three idealized views of urban America.[1] This essay pursues his notion, but not to the exclusion of small-town images rooted in other regions.

Small-town images were built around clusters of belief, attitude, and icon. The most important cluster was economic—the small town as market or place of business. Concern with small-town society (especially life-style and life cycle) and the political aspects of community were secondary. In subsequent chapters I focus on each respective cluster to show how traditional beliefs and attitudes about small towns were symbolized in the physical structure of small-town landscapes. I start with the landscape and explore the kinds of beliefs and attitudes symbolized therein in novels, photographs, and the social science literature, among other sources. I do not confront the image with the reality nor appraise degrees of objectivity so much as pursue the reverse procedure whereby the object, as icon, is seen to direct and influence the image in all its subjectivity. The coming of the automobile to small towns, and the increased geographical and social mobility it brought, altered small towns. I treat this shift from railroad to highway technology in later chapters. Increased mobility brought a change in belief and attitude as small-town people became increasingly oriented toward big-city ways.

This book is clearly an experiment. I hope to leave the reader with a renewed interest in small towns as a distinctive kind of place. I hope to do so by focusing on place images—not small towns as they actually were, so much as small towns as they were thought to be. In this essay I distill what I consider to be the prevailing images of small-town life. The book reflects time spent viewing thousands of photographs and reading and synthesizing hundreds of novels, as well as works by sociologists, anthropologists, geographers, and other social scientists. What I present is a hypothesis—a model of the American small town as place imagery. The casual reader is asked to react, to test this general view in light of his or her own experience with small towns as places. The scholar is asked to extend his or her own special capabilities and viewpoints to test my propositions, both major and minor. The questions I raise are varied. How was the American small town stereotyped as a social setting in the early twentieth century? How were these stereotypes symbolized in landscape? How did the small town change? How did small town images change?

One

Introduction

Every mature nation has its symbolic landscapes. They are part of the
iconography of nationhood, part of the shared set of ideas and
memories and feelings which bind a people together.
Donald Meinig,
The Interpretation of Ordinary Landscapes

_____

No meaning attached more readily to towns than the attribute of
smallness. Towns were by definition "small," especially when contrasted
with cities. Smallness had many dimensions: towns were limited in
physical extent and population; they supported a limited number of
economic, social, and political functions; they influenced restricted trade
hinterlands and were not well connected with places beyond. Although
most Americans shared such beliefs about towns, they were divided in
their attitudes. Small populations occupying restricted spaces were inclined to neighbor intensively, and social relationships tended to be more
highly personalized. Accordingly, some people saw small towns as friendly
places. But others saw the tyranny of forced conformity in intensive
neighboring; they felt knowing and being known too well by one's
neighbors brought alienation. As one observer writes of small towns:
"Smallness is something like an inkblot in which people find reflected
their own agendas and yearnings. Some would use smallness to get closer
to people; others farther apart."[1]

Place Images: Belief, Attitude, Icon

Beliefs and attitudes about small towns were associated with landscape features, so townscapes, or features in townscapes, served as icons
to stereotype thoughts about towns. Place images were not only imitations
or representations of landscape in the mind's eye, but, more fully, they
symbolized place as beliefs and attitudes extrapolated from suggestive
icons in the landscape. Smallness was calculated by the size of street grid
upon which a town was platted, and by the scale of Main Street as the
principal commercial area. The size and attractiveness of major buildings,

like the courthouse and railroad depot, offered additional cues. Whereas most Americans could agree upon the signatures of smallness in the landscape, attitudes differed. For some a town's few streets, small business district, and meagre tastes in architecture spelled simplicity and slowness of life in a clearly positive sense. For others the same icons spelled dullness and lack of opportunity in a clearly negative way. For most Americans some aspects of place were positive and others negative, although the overall assessment of a town, or of towns generally, was usually tipped one way or another.

In the early twentieth century, as today, place images enabled society to organize the world conceptually as geography. Images were rooted in direct experiences. But people also acted on indirect knowledge—on understandings communicated and shared as part of the popular culture. Subjectivity frequently exaggerated images and even endowed them with a touch of the mythical. Places came to symbolize human aspirations and fears magnified larger than life. Place images associated with small towns were not exceptions.

The "Myth" of the Small Town

Nowhere were the small town's mythical qualities better expressed than in the small-town novels written in the first two decades of the twentieth century. Authors like Zona Gale, Sarah Orne Jewett, Meredith Nicholson, and Booth Tarkington painted an almost bucolic picture of small town life.[2] Carl Van Doren writes of the mythical small town:

> There it lay in the mind's eye, neat, compact, organized, traditional—
> the white church with its tapering spire, the sober schoolhouse, the
> smithy of the ringing anvil, the corner grocery, the cluster of friendly
> houses, the venerable parson, the wise physician, the canny squire, the
> grasping landlord softened or outwitted in the end; the village belle,
> gossip, atheist, idiot, jovial fathers, gentle mothers, merry children;
> cool parlors, shining kitchens, spacious barns, lavish gardens,
> fragrant summer dawns, and comfortable winter evenings.[3]

Zona Gale emphasized the warmth of fellowship which close neighboring brought to small towns: "I think that in this simple basic emotion lies my joy in living in this, my village. Here, this year long, folk have been adventuring together, knowing the details of one another's lives, striving, kindling to one another's interests instead of practicing the faint morality of mere civility."[4] One of her characters exclaims: "It was the Togetherness of it. I couldn't get to sleep . . . for thinkin' about God not havin' anybody to neighbor with."[5] Such novels emphasized that sense of community especially evident in pioneer towns. The pioneer community's dependence upon mutual helpfulness muted individualistic impulses toward self-interest observed more in mature towns and cities.

The novelist used the small town as a foil to the city, especially to the metropolis where impersonal self-interest was seen as a social dominant. Towns were places to escape the cold impersonality of the city. Small towns were also used by novelists as incubators for city heroes and heroines grown to success out of humble origins. Virtues thought to be rooted in small towns were seen to nurture men and women for greatness in the city, and to promise them escape and revitalization during periods of personal crisis. As the historian Lewis Atherton writes, Americans long pretended "that log cabins surpassed mansions in producing statesmen, that agriculture and country towns constituted the proper environment for creating leaders in the arts and professions, and that pastoral pursuits contributed to virtue, the good life, and happiness."[6] The strong sense of community engendered by the inward-focused small town of the railroad era seemed to mold men and women as the impersonal city could not.

Another historian, Page Smith, argues that the small town "myth" was imposed on the town by the city.[7] Towns sought to grow and be like cities. Townspeople were thus susceptible to city ideals including the cult of the individual—the seeker of self-interest. Smith writes:

> The town at last had come to accept the city's values, and the city, having triumphed, now claimed that the values which it had imposed on the town were, in fact, the values of the town. And the city lauded the town, and sentimentalized it, and driveled over it, and called it the heart of American Democracy, the molder of men, the ancient defender of American ideals.[8]

According to Smith, urban values could be more easily appreciated in towns because of the simplicity of fewer people in smaller places. The small town was only a miniature of the city, less complex but equally urban. Towns represented a middle ground between rural and big-city life, but they were closer to the city than to the country.

The "Revolt" from the Village

Authors like Theodore Dreiser, Sherwood Anderson, Edgar Lee Masters, and Sinclair Lewis interpreted the small town with a "new realism."[9] According to Van Doren, they formulated a new movement, the "revolt from the village," which emphasized all that the "myth" had ignored—the conformity, complacency, self-righteousness, and ugly materialism of small towns.[10] The "revolt" attacked an abstraction with a counter-abstraction equally as stereotyped. Small towns were seen as parochial places isolated from the big-city mainstream; they held back more ambitious and aggressive individuals, and thus retarded progress. Since Americans accepted progress, growth, and largeness as essentially synonymous, small towns were easily viewed as backwaters and as failures. A postcard jokes "Main Street, Julian Cal. on a Busy Day," and shows the street filled with meandering cattle. Small towns were not dynamic places.

A postcard pokes fun at a California town. Small towns had been praised as ideal communities—citadels of neighborly cooperation, equality, honesty, morality. As the pendulum of opinion swung, the derision heaped on the American town was equally as stereotyped. Small towns were seen as dull, provincial, backward.

The small town became a place to escape from, rather than a place of escape. In Wallace Stegner's novel *Second Growth*, an elderly man in a Connecticut town confides to a small boy: "This is a static society Andy, a dying village. . . . In spite of everything wonderful in it, stability, laboriousness, traditions as binding as laws. . . . It's a little tribal backwater, a survival, and it doesn't lead anywhere. Whether we like it or not, the world went another way."[11] Sinclair Lewis's *Main Street* epitomized the new way of thinking. Van Doren writes: "Almost every American town had a Main Street as a matter of course. Lewis made the name a symbol and an epithet. Main Street became a symbol for narrow provincialism."[12]

Main Street is essentially the story of Carol Kennicott, college educated, urbane, and newly arrived in "Gopher Prairie" as the town doctor's new wife. Hers was a revolt against the town's destructive conformity which seemed to lead only to dullness—a dullness symbolized for Carol in the town's physical ugliness.

When Carol had walked for thirty-two minutes she had completely covered the town, east and west, north and south; and she stood at the corner of Main Street and Washington Avenue and despaired. Main Street with its two-story brick shops, its story-and-a-half wooden residences, its muddy expanse from concrete walk to walk, its huddle of Fords and lumber wagons, was too small to absorb her. The broad straight, unenticing gashes of the streets let in the grasping prairie on every side. She realized the vastness and the emptiness of the land. . . . It was not only the unsparing unapologetic ugliness and the rigid straightness which overwhelmed her. It was the plainlessness, the flimsy temporariness of the buildings, their faded unpleasant colors. The street was cluttered with electric light poles, telephone poles, gasoline pumps for motor cars, boxes of goods. Each man had built with the most valiant disregard of all the others.[13]

Guy Pollock, a "Gopher Prairie" lawyer, was the principal character in Lewis's original manuscript of *Main Street* which he entitled "Village Virus." Pollock defines for Carol the nature of the small-town virus: "It infects ambitious people who stay too long in the provinces. You'll find it epidemic among lawyers and doctors and ministers and college bred merchants—all those people who have had a glimpse of the world that thinks and laughs but have returned to their swamp."[14] The cause of the infection was easily explained: "It is an unimaginatively standardized background, a sluggishness of speech and manners, a rigid ruling of the spirit by the desire to appear respectable. It is . . . the contentment of a quiet dead, who are scornful of the living for their restless walking. It is dullness made God."[15] "Gopher Prairie" placed the highest value on the average, the normal, the predictable, and the unimaginative.[16]

The "revolt" gradually replaced the "myth" as America's dominant value system regarding small towns. Whether or not the "revolt" was imposed on the American town by dominant city ways, as Page Smith suggests the "myth" had been, it is clear that both views, along with many other interpretations of small-town life, were derived through comparison of towns with cities. With the growth of metropolitan America aided by the widespread adoption of the automobile after 1920, small towns came to be valued less for their traditional qualities and more for their communalities with big cities. Icons which had symbolized traditional values in landscape lost meaning or were assigned new meanings. New icons associated with the automobile and metropolitanism appeared in the lexicon of small-town symbolism.

The Use of Place Images

Ever since Kenneth Boulding and Daniel Boorstin first called attention to the significance of images in human behavior, social scientists have become increasingly concerned with the cognitive aspects of behavior whereby human activity is contained, indeed influenced, by the environment as it is thought to be.[17] This world of place images, called by some researchers the "behavioral environment," contains symbolic values or messages which help to cue place-appropriate behaviors.[18] Place meaning is cued by the people known to occupy and regulate a setting; by the objects that support their activities; by the timing or scheduling of those activities; and, of course, by location.[19] In part, my distilling of place images is an attempt to sort out these various aspects of place meaning as they applied to American small towns in the early twentieth century, and to assess the changes brought by the automobile through the 1950s.

During the period of rapid metropolitan growth when the American population shifted from rural places and towns to cities, there was relatively little interest among historians and social scientists in researching small towns. Scholarship which did focus on towns was largely literary. The fictional town, for its smallness, provided novelists with a manageable setting for plot and character development. The small town was well known to most Americans—a people caught in the thralls of a big-city reorientation who welcomed memories of simpler times and places in the novels they read. Only in the 1930s did writers begin to shift attention to the metropolis; and even then emphasis was placed on neighborhoods, especially ethnic neighborhoods, as a kind of small-town surrogate.[20] Page Smith writes: "Not only did most Americans live in towns . . . but the literature they read was concerned with town life; whether the town was accurately described in such fiction or whether it was transmuted by the writer's particular vision, at the very least these images of the town tell us a good deal about how many Americans viewed the small community."[21]

Wallace Stegner prefaces his novel, *Second Growth,* with the following remarks:

> The making of fiction entails the creation of places and persons with all the seeming of reality, and these places and persons, no matter how a writer tries to invent them, must be made up piecemeal from sublimitations of his own experience and his own acquaintance. The village I have tried to make is one that would exist anywhere in rural New England. . . . The people are such people as this village seems to me likely to contain, and the cultural dynamism . . . is one that has been reproduced in an endlessly changing pattern all over the United States. These people and their village took form in my mind not as portraits but as symbols.[22]

The truthfulness of such communication lies in the reader's acceptance of the author's images as plausible. To be plausible, the fictional town must agree with the reader's general picture of small towns and small-town life. This sharing of stereotypes makes the novel an extraordinary source for understanding place images.

Photography is another important source. Cameras were used to record rituals of family life, and places symbolic to family connectedness. Great similarity in photographic style and content characterized photograph albums according to the dictates of good taste and fashion. Commercial photographers were also susceptible to stereotyping. Theodore Dreiser traveling in Indiana in 1916 found commercial postcards available in every town. "I like the spirit of these towns . . . which seek out . . . the charms of the local life and embod[y] . . . them in colored prints," he wrote. "Walk into any drug or book store of any up-to-date small town, and you will find in a trice nearly every scene of importance and really learn the character and charms of the vicinity."[23]

Events recorded with a camera allowed those photographed to stand back and view themselves, their activity, and their point in time and space in a frozen likeness. In his novel *The Great Promise,* Noel Houston traces the rise of El Reno, an Oklahoma boom town. The heroine, Sawyer Tyndall, stands in her tent thinking of the previous day's lottery which had given her first draw for a town lot: "She got out a sheet of writing paper and a number of picture post cards of El Reno scenes which the photographer . . . had given her the afternoon before. On one card, showing the lottery platform at the moment . . . she was introduced . . . to the crowd, she drew an arrow to herself and lettered ME above it."[24] Photographs attached people to place and thus helped to define their social identities. As people in small towns sent postcards and shared their snapshots with relatives and friends, they communicated symbolically about their towns as places and themselves as people.

Although small in comparison to their research on cities, the work of social scientists on small towns is not without substance, especially the community case studies which sought to understand human socialization.[25] Most researchers sought to generalize about human behavior, to identify behavioral universals applicable to people in all settings. Most sought objectivity from observed consensus overtly expressed by small towners as subjects of inquiry. But much was covertly expressed in the symbolism of behavior settings. No researcher was totally divorced from consideration of small-town images rooted in landscape. Sociologist Albert Blumenthal writes in his case study of "Mineville" of the "myriad memories of blasted hopes, tragedies, successes, failures, good times, and sufferings, and departed friends and loved ones which come to the old resident as he sits upon a hillside and surveys the community. . . . Every hillside, creek, mine, street, alley, or building of consequence . . . [is] rich in associations."[26] He continues: "Formation of deeply rooted sentiments is dependent upon identification with the same objects over a long period of time. . . . The town takes on somewhat the function of a large family group; it [becomes] so intimately bound up with the resident's life that for

11

him to reject it is for him to disown a large part of himself."[27]

I am most interested in the widely shared images of the early twentieth century small town, especially the icons which are consistently repeated in the novels, photography, community case studies, and other sources of the period. Although people might use these icons differently, justifying their own beliefs and attitudes in their own terms, the icons had some consistent meaning for everyone who recognized them. People, activity, and object set in time and space served to cue beliefs about small towns, and to reinforce attitudes. Mine is a search for those symbols of small-town life in landscape.

Two

Small-Town Commerce in the Railroad Era

The East remembered generations when there had been no railroad, and had no awe of it; but here the railroads had been before time was. The towns had been staked out on barren prairie as convenient points for future train-halts.
Sinclair Lewis, *Main Street*

Towns were business propositions. Most were founded on business values which provided the stimulus for continued growth. As most were initially real estate speculations, most businessmen sought to profit from town development through land sale and the outfitting of new settlers. Successful towns, however, were based on more permanent business investments which tied local hinterlands into systems of regional and national economic organization. Towns were way stations through which the products of farms and mines moved to market. Small towns also served as distribution points through which local areas were supplied with goods and services which originated elsewhere. Small-town Main Streets symbolized these basic commercial impulses.

The railroad was vital to small-town business in the early twentieth century. Coastal and river towns might survive without a railroad, but few thrived. The railroad was absolutely necessary for inland towns. Towns born before the railroad died when they did not obtain railroad connections, and new towns were stillborn when plans for railroad links evaporated. The railroad was the small town's lifeline; it nurtured the town within a matrix of connected places.

Land Office Business

Speculation in real estate was especially evident in the new "boom" towns of the early twentieth century staked out along the railroads of the Midwest and West. Surveyed lots oriented to a grid of streets spoke of land speculation. The picture which Noel Houston paints of El Reno, Oklahoma, in *The Great Promise,* was typical. Lottery specials brought people to the point chosen on the railroad for the new town: "Each train looked as if giant bees had swarmed on it. Men stood on the cowcatcher, sprawled on the tender, huddled on the roofs of the coaches. Wherever a foothold and handhold could be obtained there clung a man." Houston continues: "Every hour another train dumped a thousand more people into the jam-pack. Ringing the town was a vast encampment of farm conveyances and canvas tents, standing in groves of cookfire smoke rising straight from the prairie into the motionless hot air." Sawyer Tyndall, Houston's heroine, walked the periphery of the town site just prior to the drawing for lots. She saw "piles of new, yellow lumber. Many wagons were being loaded high from the piles. Standing about were a number of frame buildings, newly erected and mounted on solid barrel-like wheels to be rolled to permanent locations."[1]

After the lottery had been completed, the town sprung to life—its constituent pieces rapidly inserted into a new townscape.

> Out from the encampment . . . rolled a one-story frame building with a two-story front, drawn by six teams. The sun flashed on a window pane as a carpenter riding inside fitted a sash. Across the high front an uncompleted relettered sign reading GOTTLEIB'S MERCAN blazoned wetly. A painter carrying a ladder and bucket walked alongside, ready to resume his lettering as soon as the building reached its destination.[2]

The first day of filing for lots at Gregory, South Dakota (1909). Boom towns appeared in the early twentieth century in Oklahoma on what had been Indian land, in the Dakotas where a wheat craze reigned, or wherever new railroad lines were constructed. A surveyed plat of land, a sales office with map and aggressive salesmen, ready financing, and ease of outfitting and supply were the necessary ingredients for successful town development.

A similar scene is depicted in a photograph of Gregory, South Dakota, another boom town of the twentieth century's first decade. Pictured is the land office still askew in the middle of Main Street, the business district filled in around it. Adjacent is the enterprising business of Samuel Chilton, a land "locator." Chilton also operated a bank, furniture store, and undertaking establishment: caskets supplemented the furniture, which outfitted the new settlers who travelled light to claim new farms or town lots. Many settlers bought their land from Chilton with bank loans. The automobile standing in the street not only facilitated the business of selling land, but also served to symbolize that Chilton's various businesses were thoroughly modern. A Mrs. Melcher sits in the car's front seat. Like Houston's heroine of El Reno, Mrs. Melcher is shown with deed in hand, the winner of the first draw for town lots. Gregory, like El Reno, was a place for fresh starts—a place of opportunity.

A booster's day parade in Gregory, South Dakota (circa 1915). The first decades of the twentieth century were prosperous times for America's small towns. Business optimism ran high, and many towns considered themselves no less than the embryos of large metropolises.

"Watch Gregory Grow" reads the banner strung across the street in another photograph taken several years later. The Samuel Chiltons of Gregory have produced a viable town. Twelve automobiles are pictured parading on a local "Booster's Day." Two more cars are parked at the curb, and only one horse is evident. Concrete sidewalks and electric power lines are further symbols of progress, although the street is yet to be paved and lighted. The two-story brick and masonry facades symbolize a viable commerce. Here is the Midwestern "Main Street" in a new, raw, frontier

15

country. The photographer has taken to the rooftops to picture candidly a staged event. Yet the wide panorama is clearly necessary to capture the array of symbols intended to impress viewers with the prosperity Gregory has produced.

Few towns experienced such explosive birth as recorded by the novelist and photographer in El Reno and Gregory respectively. Nonetheless, every town had its speculative stage which promised an exaggerated future. As the speculators and other town builders withdrew (many to replay their roles elsewhere), a more permanent business community asserted leadership with less extravagant claims for future growth. Bankers, wholesalers, and retail merchants settled down to the day-to-day business of attracting local farm trade, promoting whatever local industry looked promising, or seeing to the development of local mineral resources. In the less exuberant climate of "business as usual" the town still looked to the railroad as the vital lifeline. The railroad was no longer an umbilical cord offering temporary sustenance, but a true artery of commerce linking the town and its area in a permanent relationship to regional and national markets.

The Depot

The railroad depot stood at the center of a town in a symbolic, if not functional, sense. As the depot was the principal interface with the outside world, travelers and freight moved constantly through its portals. Here was the telegraph office with instant communication to outside places. At train time the depot was charged with expectation. Travelers waited anxiously and loafers collected to survey the "coming and goings" as in the photograph of the depot at Sadorus, Illinois. Booth Tarkington writes of the fictional "Plattville" station in his novel, *The Gentleman From Indiana:*

> On the station platforms there are always two or three wooden packing boxes, apparently marked for travel, but they are sacred from disturbance and remain on the platform forever. . . . They serve to enthrone a few station loafers, who look out from under their hat brims at the faces in the car windows with the languid scorn a permanent fixture always has for a transient, and the pity an American feels for a fellow-being who does not live in his town.[3]

Through the railroad depot came newlyweds departing on honeymoon trips, school classes off to the city, young men departing for war. There arrived traveling salesmen with valises filled with samples, wives returning from shopping excursions loaded down with bundles, and coffins of the deceased returned home for burial.

The depot was one of the finest buildings of the town—perhaps, as

The railroad depot at Sadorus, Illinois (1918). The railroad connected the town and its hinterland with regional and national markets. The photograph shows idlers gathered in anticipation of an afternoon train—caught by an amateur photographer, herself about to depart on vacation with a new camera.

View of Larned, Kansas, from the railroad depot (circa 1924). Views along the railroad were generally unattractive until the traveler stepped from the train at the depot. There, in many towns, the full display of Main Street was visible—a classic scene for the postcard photographer.

Sinclair Lewis suggests, even its "final aspiration of architecture."[4] Stations varied according to railroad company, and the towns along a given line usually shared common, look-alike centerpieces. The arrival of a train brought absolute commotion. Teenagers made last-minute dashes in front of the locomotive. Mothers gathered small children to them as the engine swished by, hissing and tooting and looking, as one observer put it, much like a "Shakespearean army" rushing on stage.[5] The depot was small-town theater at its active best.

The depot and its environs formed the visitor's preliminary impression of a town. Sometimes adjacent coal yards, grain elevators, and similar utilitarian scenes spoiled the visitor's first view of a town. In some towns Main Street literally faced the railroad at the depot, offering the visitor a fine prospect for first impressions. Such was the case in Larned, Kansas.

Main Street

Larned spread before the visitor as he or she looked up Main Street from the depot. There was the Electric Hotel, small and none too modern despite its name. The hotel served railroad employees and town bachelors, for its rooms were cheap. Better-to-do salesmen, affluent businessmen, and tourists stayed up the street at the town's newer hostelry, built closer to the town's best residential area. Before the automobile era with its taxicabs, horse-drawn hacks met each passenger train to hasten travelers the length of the business district.

Main Street was an enclosed setting. Building facades made two distinct edges which emphasized the linearity of the street. Part of a larger rectilinear grid of streets, the Main Street of most towns stretched uninterrupted to the horizon. Nothing anchored the view either up or down the street. Equally lacking was a sense of nodality beyond the clustering of banks and the higher class "department" stores at a principal intersection, unless there was a courthouse square.

Although there were few pretenses to beauty and relatively little effort made to blend the architecture of one building with another, most Main Streets at the beginning of the twentieth century fit together as attractive, if not distinctive, business settings. The form of each Main Street was a unique configuration with buildings of different sizes, shapes, and silhouettes.[6] Nonetheless, the availability of a limited range of building material in any given place, the use of common construction techniques, and the popularity of a few architectural styles in any given period brought visual cohesion to most small-town business districts.

Building scale, the mix of buildings of different sizes, use of materials, and the details of architectural decoration varied regionally—usually

18

as a function of the period of town development and the size of town. Multistory brick buildings typified larger places whereas one- and two-story buildings, often with false fronts, characterized smaller places. New towns tended to be built of wood and older towns of brick. Across the northern tier of states, from New England to the Pacific Northwest, frame construction predominated even in the larger centers. Brick construction typified the Middle Atlantic states, the lower Midwest, and the upper South, even in the smaller centers. Adobe and simulated adobe buildings of masonry and plaster were common in much of New Mexico and southern California. The use of fieldstone in upstate New York and "post rock" in Kansas made for distinctive streetscapes in those localities.

Buildings were related functionally to streets in a single, very simple formula. Most buildings were long, narrow, rectangular boxes of one, two, or three stories with one narrow side facing the street. Display windows served to attract customers into sales spaces organized perpendicular to the sidewalk. In the typical grocery store, customers found shelves along each wall, and two long counters crowded with cash registers, scales, and other paraphernalia of business. Barrels and packing cases stood open for inspection in the center of the room.

Grocery store at Harrisburg, Illinois (1920). This store was typical of Main Street America in the first decades of the twentieth century. A commercial photographer has been hired to record opening day activities. The owner and his clerks strike an obvious pose.

Although Main Street was constructed to accommodate the wagons and the other vehicles which farmers drove to town, it was essentially a

Hitching rail in a small Wisconsin town (circa 1910). Farmers drove to town to trade. Surplus farm products, such as the chickens and milk carried in the wagons pictured, were bartered for the copper boilers, axes, cloth, dresses, and the other goods displayed in the store windows.

The square at Angola, Indiana (1905). A young housewife and mother writes to her brother on the back of the postcard: "This is a picture of the east side of the publick [sic] square. The building with Patterson's sign over it is one of our buildings." The abstract office and the law office suggest that the courthouse was nearby.

pedestrian place. Farmers tied their teams to the hitching posts which lined each curb, and walked from store to store. Town residents also walked to do their shopping, for most stores offered delivery service and town customers were not burdened with carrying packages home. Sidewalk improvement was a critical concern; by World War I most towns had replaced the wooden planking downtown with concrete. Sidewalks in most southern and western towns were covered with wooden, metal, or canvas sunshades. The more enterprising merchants in other parts of the country installed retractable awnings. Sidewalk covers served to protect merchandise displayed on public walks, and reduce the sun's glare and heat within the stores. Many towns, usually the smaller places, maintained rows of shade trees along business streets, as around the square in Angola, Indiana.

More competitive merchants erected highly visible, if not garish, signs. Angola's "Good Goods" store caught the customer's attention blocks away. Nonetheless, early in the twentieth century most signs along American Main Streets were geared more to nearby observation. William L. White remembers the Main Street of his Kansas hometown:

> The stores were one-story buildings with false fronts. Most of them had corrugated-iron sunshields which ran from the store front to the sidewalks, supported there by two iron pillars and casting a welcome rectangle of shade over the display windows and over the wide sidewalk. The store windows sometimes displayed a few pyramids of canned or packaged merchandise in them, or perhaps only the colored cardboard cut-outs furnished by the wholesale houses, showing a pretty girl sipping a soft drink, or flaky doughnuts baked with somebody's cottonseed oil.[7]

Retail stores dominated Main Street business. Professional offices were located upstairs as were apartments, some occupied by the families who ran the businesses below. The spectrum of goods and services available on Main Street was largely a function of town size which was, in turn, related to the size of its trade hinterland. Larger towns offered more goods and services to larger trade areas. About 1900, grocery, hardware and implement, furniture, drug, and clothing stores could be found in even the smallest towns—along with restaurants and bakeries, saloons (except where antisaloon laws prevailed), barbershops, pool halls, blacksmith shops, and livery stables. Most stores stressed convenience goods or sold a range of specialty items. Price Evan's furniture store and undertaking establishment in Homer, Illinois, also sold sewing machines and pianos. Such clustering of goods and services was necessary in the smaller towns where the market for any one item was limited.

Main Street in Homer, Illinois (1909). Photographers on Main Street were still sufficiently rare to seize the absolute attention of two idlers.

Larger towns featured specialty stores with relatively narrow merchandise lines. Food stores specialized in groceries, meats, or fruits and vegetables to the exclusion of other products. Implements, carriage, harness, paint, bicycle, and gun sales were usually separated from general hardware sales. Music stores, book shops, and stores specializing either in women's or men's fashions (or separate lines of clothing such as hats or shoes) were common. Although banks were found in towns of all sizes, those in the larger places often served as clearing houses for banks in nearby, smaller centers.

The mix of different enterprises along Main Street was usually random except at the high-rent intersection. There the most profitable businesses occupied the costliest land—real estate priced for its centrality and high accessibility within the business district and town. In Gilman City, Missouri, two banks, a department store, and a drugstore defined the principal intersection at Main and Cook Streets.

Different businesses were intermixed along most Main Streets. In Homer, Illinois, Pete's Confectionery Ice Cream Parlor occupied the building next door to Evans's Furniture Store. Beyond the ice cream parlor was a drugstore, a soft goods store, and a bank. Thus the sights, sounds, and smells varied as the resident or visitor walked the length of Main Street. Madison Cooper describes Main Street's variety in "Sironia," Texas: "He liked the smells here: the moth balls of textiles, the paint and grease of farm implements, the earthiness of vegetables, the

22

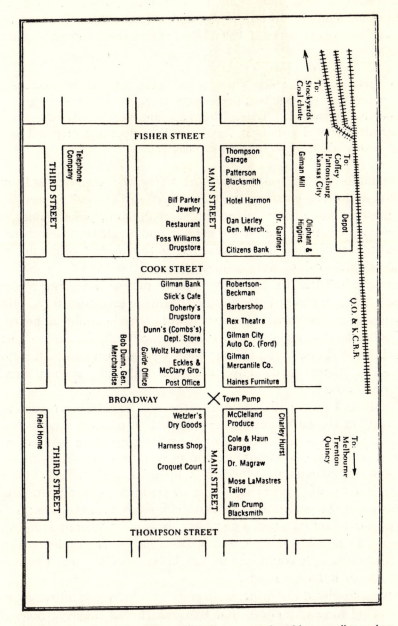

Main Street at Gilman City, Missouri (1910), as remembered by a small-town boy. Here was a mixture of businesses, including some not traditional to Main Street—a movie house, several garages, and an automobile dealer. Reprinted from *Hurry Home Wednesday: Growing up in a Small Missouri Town, 1905–1921*, by Loren Reid, by permission of the University of Missouri Press. Copyright 1978 by the Curators of the University of Missouri.

leather of saddles, the food smells, making an unmistakable alloy of their own."[8]

Barbershops, sometimes called "tonsorial parlors," were often located in basements of hotels, bank buildings, or other large structures. Access was by way of stairs cut down into the sidewalk, and protected by a metal railing.

> The barbershop was a man's world, and ladies hurried by to escape the ogling and raucous laughter evident through the flimsy facade. Cigar smoke, sweet tart scent of bay rum, and stench of lavishly applied tonic greeted visitors as they opened the door and prepared to match wits and stories with their cronies.[9]

In Ferdinand Reyher's novel, *I Heard them Sing,* the town barber thought of his shop as nothing less than the "Capitol of the Town." Everything of importance originated there "from the baseball team, poker games, fireman's festival, sociables church and lay . . . and magic lantern lectures, to larger matters pertaining to Progress. Or if they didn't originate in his shop the original notions were refined [t]here."[10]

The pool hall had its distinctive role to play as a loafing place for older men, and as a place of clandestine adventure for young boys. Homer Croy writes of his fictional Missouri town: "Inside could be heard the click of balls, the shaking of dice in a leather cup, [and] the clink of money in a machine of chance. . . . On the walls were pictures from the *Police Gazette* and . . . post cards showing women with scant clothes, holding bouquets of flowers."[11]

Saloons and pool halls comprised the less respectable precincts on Main Street. In the larger towns, a small district of such establishments might characterize the railroad end of Main Street or the portion of Main Street beyond the tracks. Gambling and prostitution thrived in the larger places between infrequent crackdowns by town authorities. This was especially true of mining towns, where single men formed an unusually large portion of the population. In Telluride, Colorado, the ground floor of each bordello housed a bar, a gambling room, a restaurant (run by one of the town's Chinese families), and a dance hall. "The orchestras, considered first-class, were comprised of 'alcoholic musicians who had drifted in at the end of unhappy roads.'"[12]

Banks epitomized the respectable end of Main Street, although many authors would have us believe that banks harbored bigger crooks than saloons and bordellos.[13] Banks were the instruments by which towns could be controlled. Lewis Atherton writes: "A new and acquisitive society emphasized basic aims. [Money] meant so many hogs or cattle or acres of land to the farmer; it measured store goods and business buildings for the merchant. In handling it, the banker manipulated the symbols which identified the successful men."[14] Bank buildings were built to symbolize wealth and success. Novelist Larry Woiwode describes the bank at "Hyatt" in North Dakota as the only building made of brick and the only one that even hinted at opulence: "Flat stone pillars flank its entrance. Four wide steps of stone lead to a pair of doors so heavy they're hard to push open."[15] Banks drew strength from appearing strong.

Lodge halls were among the more architecturally refined buildings: in Webster, New York, the mansard-roofed Masonic Lodge, with retail space on the first floor, presented a silhouette equal that of the nearby bank.

Main Street in Webster, New York (1907). The message on the back, to Miss Adele Murphy, reads: "We are on our way back from a trip to Webster. How are you all at Waupaca? I think of you often. Love to Mama. Auntie Chad." Postcard views stereotyped American small-town scenes in association with warm, intimate messages for and about family and friends.

Opera houses were also impressive buildings. Wright's Opera House in Douglas, Kansas, gave Main Street an elaborate facade. The opera house was a town's entertainment center in the days before motion pictures. Rose Wilder Lane writes in her novel, *Old Home Town:*

Upstairs, above one of the stores, was the G.A.R. Hall. Above another store was the Opera House, where at long intervals towns-people had the treat of hearing a lecture illustrated with magic lantern slides, or of seeing trained dogs and listening to tunes played on the musical glasses. When blind Boone came to town, he played a piano in the opera house, and every winter the Ladies' Aid gave oyster-suppers there.[16]

Wright's Opera House in Douglas, Kansas (1909). Certain landmarks stood out on Main Street to attract the photographer's attention. Wright's featured a cast-iron front which simulated a heavy stone facade.

The courthouse square at Clarion, Iowa (circa 1918). Views taken from the town water tower were part of the commercial photographer's stock in trade. Business buildings dominated Clarion's square on three sides, with the nearest intersection the prime business address. ''Back of the square'' was still residential—a logical place for chain stores and various automobile-oriented businesses to locate later.

According to Atherton, the term *opera house* was used in deference to small-town moral sensibilities, "operas being sufficiently distant and uplifting to escape the damning influence of the word 'theatre.'"[17]

> A stairway carved with the initials of patrons and small boys led to the second story . . . where kitchen chairs, removable for dances, rose tier by tier on a series of platforms until they reached the ceiling. On entering the room, patrons immediately noticed the combined odor of chewing gum, dried tobacco juice, heated foul air, and grease-paint perfume, the seductive opera house smell.[18]

The Square

The business districts of many towns focused on squares, especially courthouse squares as in Clarion, Iowa.[19] There the courthouse, located in an otherwise open block, visually dominated the town center. Towns which unsuccessfully had sought court seats were often left with completely open squares filled only with a monument or, perhaps, a bandstand as in Rose Wilder Lane's town.[20] Business districts in such towns often spread out along a nearby Main Street, as if to ignore the town's failure to become a seat of government. Courthouse squares, on the other hand, were traffic generators and, accordingly, business generally concentrated around them. In towns selected as court seats after Main Street developed, courthouses were usually located away from downtown.

William Faulkner's fictional Mississippi town of "Jefferson" focused on a courthouse square: the courthouse in its grove the center; quadrangular around it, the stores, the offices of the lawyers and doctors and dentists, the lodge-rooms and auditoriums above them; the four broad diverging avenues straight as plumb-lines, in the four directions, becoming the network of roads and by-roads for the whole county.[21] Both novelists and social scientists have viewed the square as an icon of community. Faulkner writes: "The courthouse was the nucleus of the town, the symbol of civilized society—church, courthouse, school, in that order, with the courthouse the 'catalyst,' without which there was no town."[22] Geographer Edward Price observes: "The nuclear functions of town and country are embodied in a nuclear frame—in the center the cupolated tower with its four-faced clock striking the hours; then the courthouse building; the unbuilt void with its park, fence, and circulating lines; the town's business district, the residential part of the town; finally the rural county."[23]

Courthouse squares functioned as ritual places on ceremonial occasions. Celebrations and political rallies focused there. On ordinary days a male resident was very likely to encounter friends on or around the square. Every square had its idlers. In *The Gentleman from Indiana,* Booth Tark-

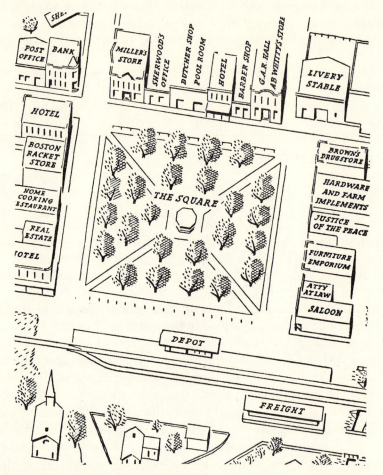

The square in Rose Wilder Lane's *Old Home Town.* Novels perpetuated stereotyped views of small towns although few novelists provided their readers with maps or diagrams. Source: Rose Wilder Lane, *Old Home Town* (New York: Longmans, Green, 1935), end papers.

ington writes: "When the sun grew too hot for the dry goods box whittlers in front of the stores around the square and the occupants of the corner, they would go across and drape themselves over the courthouse fence, under the trees, and leisurely carve their initials on the top board."[24] The courthouse itself was definitely a male-oriented place. Ross Lockridge writes in *Raintree County* that any man might go into it or hang around outside of it, jetting tobacco juice. But a woman went into the courthouse only for a very special purpose." "Raintree County's" courthouse smelled of tobacco and urine, "the immemorial odor of all American courthouses, the masculine odor of civic probity, justice, and official function."[25]

The courthouse was architecturally the most elaborate building in a

28

town, if the railroad depot did not claim that honor. For Esther, the young heroine in Lockridge's novel,

> the new courthouse was by far the most impressive building [she] had ever seen. Below and behind the great tower . . . the main building was a strong rectangle of brick trimmed with stone at the corners, doors, windows, and eaves. The main entrance was through the base of the tower, where justice, a life-sized woman with scales, stood in a niche above the door. The tower rose to a height of 110 feet, having at the top a foursided steep roof, dwindling to a small observation platform, fenced, from which stood a masted American flag.[26]

The Horse in the Landscape

The horse was central to a town's geography. Farmers used horse-drawn wagons to bring crops to market; they used carriages and wagons to patronize local stores. Most Main Streets were wide enough to accommodate turning teams, and business streets were usually lined with hitching rails. Most squares had at least one watering trough. Evidence of the horse was everywhere, from the droppings swarming with flies to the ruts cut deep in the streets by narrow-wheeled wagons.

Feed and sale barns, livery stables, and blacksmith shops were often located on the side streets off Main Street. The typical livery stable was a large, barnlike building with oversized doors to accommodate wheeled

A new wagon on Main Street, town unknown (circa 1910). A farmer and his son stop before a photographer's studio to have a "likeness" made of their new, store-bought wagon. Horse-drawn vehicles tied farm to town in the preautomobile scheme of local geography.

vehicles. Typically, a small office near the door contained a battered desk, a potbellied stove, several chairs, and a cot. On the walls were posted signs expounding the merits of liniments, announcing farm sales, or stating terms of rental:

> Whip light,
> Drive slow,
> Pay cash,
> Before you go.[27]

Blacksmith shop in a Missouri town (circa 1920). Blacksmith shops were strictly utilitarian. The noise, smoke, and animals relegated most shops to back alleys or side streets away from Main Street stores. Nonetheless, pride of ownership saw this shop widely advertised by picture postcard.

Salesmen rented horses and carriages to haul sample cases on trips out into the hinterland. Fancy buggies and sleighs could be rented for special social outings. Town doctors kept their horses and rigs at the liveries for ready use. The funeral home's hearse was usually stored there, as were the hotel hacks and the town's street sprinklers. A livery stable mingled the smells of horse manure with those of harness oil, grease, feed, and hay.

Stalls were to the rear, from which horses were led up cleated ramps to the main floor for hitching. A second-floor loft over the stables facilitated the forking down of hay used for feed. Harness for each animal hung on wooden pegs at the front of his stall. Somewhere in the building was the washroom where buggies were washed and wheels were greased. Curry combs, hair clippers, sponges, axle grease, harness soap, and pitch forks were scattered through the building.[28]

The livery stable was another male-dominated place for loafing and gossip.

The streets of most towns were unimproved save, perhaps, for Main Street. In wet weather streets were rutted and gouged with potholes, with water standing everywhere. In dry weather dust covered everything despite the efforts of the sprinkler wagons which regularly traversed the town. Booth Tarkington writes of "Plattville": "In winter, Main Street was a series of frozen gorges and hummocks; in fall and spring, a river of mud; in summer, a continuing dust heap."[29]

By World War I most towns had replaced gas and kerosene lamps with electric arc or electric bulb devices. There was no real need for extensive lighting. Farmers who travelled by horse and wagon came only during the day. Stores were open only during daylight hours, although on a summer's evening that might mean eight or nine o'clock. Before World War I most Main Streets were lined with power and telephone lines which, along with the street lights, helped to integrate the street visually. Such accouterments symbolized local progress in a new technological age.

Vehicular traffic moved at a leisurely pace. A person could walk freely on most streets at the busiest times of day. The ultimate small-town prank was to blockade Main Street, as at Homer, Illinois, on Halloween night 1908. The split-rail fence was allowed to stand through the next day as a curiosity, so little traffic was disrupted. Danger increased when interurban streetcars began to compete with horses on Main Street, as at

"After Hallowe'en '08" in Homer, Illinois. Pity the farmer forced to retrieve his fence from town. The prank was relived for years through local storytelling; such events, as shared experiences, heightened the sense of belonging to a town.

Stonington, Connecticut. Interurban cars connected small towns with nearby cities. The highest density of lines developed in the Northeast and in the Midwest.[30] The cars loaded both passengers and freight in the middle of small-town Main Streets, with converted storefronts usually serving as depots.

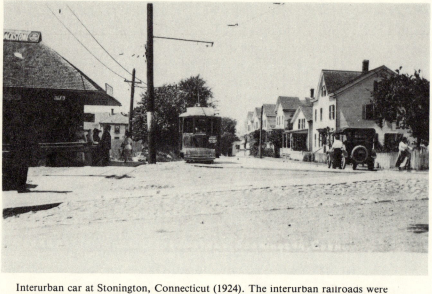

Interurban car at Stonington, Connecticut (1924). The interurban railroads were short-lived. By 1930 most had succumbed to the competition of automobiles, buses, and trucks. Stonington's interurban depot was also a gasoline station—a sign of things to come.

Along the Tracks

Railroads created distinctive landscapes in their immediate environs. The view along the Wabash Railroad at West Unity, Ohio, was typical. The passenger depot, freight station, water tank, coaling platform, tool shed, signalling towers, and switching tracks marked the property of the railroad company. Adjacent were wholesale and warehousing establishments to handle farm produce and to supply both town and country with fuel, building materials, and other bulk commodities. Carol Kennicott's first glimpse of "Gopher Prairie" in Sinclair Lewis's *Main Street* was of such a landscape: "Now the train was passing the elevator, the grim storage-tanks for oil, a creamery, a lumber-yard, a stock-yard muddy and trampled and stinking."[31]

In the Midwest and West, grain elevators dominated the small-town skyline. In the South a cotton gin, a tobacco warehouse, or a sugar refinery might dominate a railroad right-of-way. Before the age of electric

32

The railroad at West Unity, Ohio (1915). Utility prevailed along the railroad tracks as there was little room for the picturesque where grain elevators, lumberyards, and factories were concerned. New trees had been planted around the depot—perhaps a token effort by the local garden club.

Grain elevators at Mott, North Dakota (1910). In the Midwest and West the grain elevators signalled towns at intervals of five to seven miles along the railroad lines. The back of the postcard reads: ''Hello Roy. We have had some fine rains and it is hot as blazes. The crops are growing and so is Mott. Leslie.''

refrigeration, icehouses were common along the tracks everywhere in the South and in many towns elsewhere. In ''Good Union,'' Mary King's fictional Oklahoma town,

> the frayed planks of the icehouse porch were wet and cool to the soles of . . . bare feet. People kept watermelons in the icehouse. When the heavy door swung open, a cold foggy breath would slide out and spread around. . . . Men, squatting on their heels in the striped shade, would split the ripe melons with their pocket knives, spear a red hunk on the end of the blade, and pop it into their mouths, spitting the black seeds . . . the talk never stopping.[32]

Ice house at White Hall, Illinois (circa 1910). The kinds of warehouses and processing plants along the railroad tracks varied from one section of the country to another—cotton and tobacco in the South, corn and wheat in the Midwest, citrus fruit in Florida and California.

Novelists worked with the railroad landscape in various ways. Mary King used the railroad to establish a sense of commonality between towns, as one character looks at ''Good Union'' for the first time: ''Somehow, it looked familiar. There were the tank cars drawn up on a siding, the yellow depot, the yellow toilets marked 'Ladies' and 'Gents,' the yellow section house. And there was the cotton gin.''[33] Sinclair Lewis criticized the railroad as overly functional and sterile: a railroad cut off ''Gopher Prairie'' from its nearby lake for utility, and not aesthetics, ruled the day. Nonetheless, his heroine Carol Kennicott found the activity and excitement of the mills and factories a pleasant contrast to the dullness and inactivity of the remainder of the town.

34

She lost her loneliness in the activity of the village industries—the railroad-yards with a freight-train switching, the wheat-elevator, oil-tanks, a slaughter-house with blood marks on the snow, the creamery with the sleds of farmers and piles of milk-cans, an unexplained stone hut labeled 'Danger—Powder Stored Here.' The jolly tombstone-yard . . . the planing mill, with the smell of fresh pine shavings and the burr of circular saws. . . . The latter was a relief to Carol after months of smug houses.[34]

Mill and Mine

Not all small towns were exclusively trade centers. Some were predominantly factory towns, as in southern New England and in the Carolina Piedmont. Some were almost totally dependent on local mines, as in the coalfields of Pennsylvania, West Virginia, Kentucky, and Indiana. Most towns had at least some kind of manufacturing rooted in the processing of local agricultural products. Some developed special relationships with agriculture, the location of a plant stimulating growth of an agricultural specialty region. Hoopeston, Illinois, for example, developed as a sweet-corn canning center. Sweet-corn cultivation came to dominate agriculture in the town's hinterland. Small plants producing tin cans and cardboard boxes also located in Hoopeston, making the town a small manufacturing center. Early in the twentieth century most small-town factories employed fewer than thirty workers. Working space was organized

A sweet-corn canning plant at Hoopeston, Illinois (1921). Hoopeston built its industry on agriculture, creating a crop specialty area in its hinterland where none had existed before.

35

A cotton seed mill at Cuero, Texas (circa 1910). Smoke billowing from factory stacks signified prosperity in small towns just as in big cities.

Cotton mill workers at Cuero, Texas (circa 1910). Cheap labor was usually what attracted industrial plants to small towns. Children, women, and men worked long hours to tend presses, power looms, and other machines often under hazardous conditions. Photographers visited factories to take group pictures, and returned to sell the photographs to employees.

36

vertically on two or three floors. Before the age of electrical machinery, power—generated by water turbines or steam engines and distributed by belt—was used most efficiently in vertically organized buildings. Factories were compact, taking up relatively little space.

Industry at Cuero, Texas, was also supported by local agriculture. The cotton seed mill at Cuero employed girls and young women. Daughters of farm families and immigrant families (whose fathers and sons also worked in the mills) represented an inexpensive source of unskilled labor in towns across the United States. When factories were successfully established, town hinterlands were partially redefined as areas from which laborers were drawn.

Towns were constantly beguiled by promoters who promised large numbers of jobs and steady town growth, should communities subsidize construction of a factory. More often than not, such ventures ended in disaster as communities squandered their investment capital. Hoopeston's experiment with canning was a success, but the attempted industrialism in Angola, Indiana, flopped. Newell Simms, a sociologist, studied Angola before World War I, calling the town "Aton." A commercial club had been formed, and raised seventy thousand dollars to build a small plant to attract a manufacturer of refrigerators. "Under the enthusiasm of booming the town, stock sold 'like hot cakes' though nobody knew whether the company had been a success or would continue to be. Purchase of stock in the company became a craze that swept the town."[35] Newspaper editorials, political speeches, and gossip all exalted the proposition: "It is believed the community is the cheapest place in which to live in the U.S.; that it is the most democratic; the most temperate; the most law-abiding; that its college is of peculiar merit; and its churches of unusual excellence. Much is said of the beauty and healthfulness of the place in comparison with others."[36] But in the final analysis the town had been swindled. "The company was bankrupt, had played a 'skin game' on 'Aton,' and completely buncoed its citizens." All efforts to boost "Aton" industrially ceased. The new era had failed to materialize.[37] Small towns like Angola failed to become cities, but at least they tried.

Although sociologists might report that small-town people wanted factories and the trappings of the industrial age, most novelists saw in industrialism the antithesis of small-town life. Mills were seen as impersonal, alien places of machines against which the warmth of home and hearth could be contrasted. Writing of "Bardsville," Robert Penn Warren describes a southern mill town after World War I:

> Across the creek are the long, new, raw-brick structures of the war
> plant set in the gashed and still red-wounded clay, one of the tin-bright

37

stacks still releasing unwaveringly the black smoke in a single column to an improbable height in the motionless, heat-benumbed air. And there are the dilapidated piles of the old furniture factory (which made ammunition boxes for the war), the coal yards on the patch of grassed earth, which glitters like mica, and the tracks, switches, and sidings exposed among the jumble, like a tangle of disected nerves, to glitter too, and quiver in the incandescent light. You cannot see the stone ruin of the old mill that stands at the other end of the bridge. But you do see, beyond the creek, flung down beyond the tracks, the shanties, trailers, and prefabricated houses of the war workers, and beyond that the shanties of nigger town which straggle up the hill, with washing here and there hanging abjectly on crazy lines like improvised flags of surrender among the ruins.[38]

The typical mine stood stark and foreboding in the landscape, the slag and the cast-off equipment accumulating around the shaft head. The tipple, the washhouse, and the smokestacks dominated many a coal town such as Buckner, Illinois. Like factories, mines were often short-lived. In a reminiscence of his hometown, Jack Conroy writes:

Monkey Nest coal-mine tipple stood ten years; its dirt dump grew from a diminutive hillock among the scrub oaks to the height of a young mountain . . . the dump dominated Monkey Nest camp like an Old World cathedral towering over peasant huts . . . . [The tipple] was like a gallows . . . the cage cable dangled from the cathead like a hangman's rope.[39]

Coal mine at Buckner, Illinois (circa 1910). The coal company sunk the mine at Buckner, laid out the town, and opened the first store. Many Lithuanians and other eastern Europeans settled in the town. Both the coal and the profits from the mining flowed to Chicago where postcards of the company's facilities were circulated as advertising.

View of Tonapah, Nevada (circa 1910). Main Street crouches at the foot of a mining landscape. The town was not entirely of its own making, for many buildings were prefabricated in distant factories and shipped to Tonapah for fast assembly. Small houses lined the alley back of Main Street next to a blacksmith shop, carriage shop, and wood lot. There was little pretense at beauty in Tonapah.

Workers in a Pennsylvania oil field. The message on the back of the postcard reads: "This is a picture I had taken at work. The big fellow is my tooldresser. I will send you one of my wife and I in next letter. This will give you some idey [sic] of the oil works if you never seen any."

Mine tipples and slag heaps loom over the town of Tonapah, Nevada, in a photograph taken about 1910. Western mining towns were usually very isolated, an entire world in microcosm. Like lumber towns in the northern Midwest and Pacific Northwest, they were not surrounded by vigorous farming populations. Phil Strong writes of "Birora's" isolation in *The Iron Mountain*: "Not many people left Birora by train; not many arrived there, so that two or three dingy coaches came in twice a day, passing among a few hundred fifty-ton ore gondolas."[40] Mining totally dominated such towns. At "Birora," signs of iron were everywhere; everything was coated with a dried salmon dust. Mining towns were literally built overnight. Buildings appeared to be flimsy—seemingly more temporary than in farm and factory towns. Mining-town architecture was usually of a single vernacular style, and thus lacked a visual sense of historical depth. The appearance of uniformity was especially true of company-owned towns.

Mining towns were male-dominated in their entirety. Life was organized around the mine and its work. Physical strength and technical know-how were admired in men who wrenched coal, iron, copper, gold, silver, or oil from the ground. Utilitarian values predominated. Photographers who journeyed to mining towns expended much effort picturing work and workers.

Conclusion

Whether in a mining town, a mill town, or a farm trade center, the railroad was vital to small-town existence in the early twentieth century. The town joined local products to the national system of exchange. It served as a distribution point for the goods and services which originated at a distance. It was not surprising that new towns were laid out with railroads at their centers, and that old towns were substantially intruded upon and reorganized by the arrival of a railroad line. Small towns displayed much variety as to the specifics of layout. In some towns Main Street paralleled the railroad; in others it crossed the railroad, bisected by the tracks. In river and coastal towns originally oriented to water, Main Street and the railroad sometimes appeared to be totally unrelated. Nonetheless, a general model of the railroad town of the early twentieth century is possible.

The small town was oriented to a railroad line which formed one of its principal axes for commercial development. Facilities for the bulk exchange of commodities and the processing of raw materials were located along the railroad right-of-way. Here also were a town's factories and its

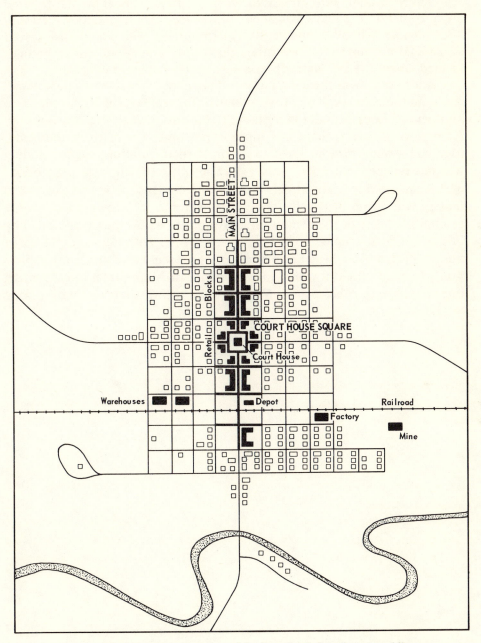

A hypothetical small town: commercial orientation before the automobile age.

mines. The landscape which emerged was utilitarian and largely devoid of the picturesque.

Main Street formed the other axis for development. It was usually centered on a single intersection or, as in the hypothetical model, focused on a courthouse square. Business blocks were punctuated with land-marks—hotels, banks, lodge halls, opera houses. The courthouse served as a visual anchor as well as traffic generator. The depot was sometimes located where the two axes of commercial development crossed.

Main Street was the most important symbol of small-town commerce. Railroad landscapes looked very much the same from one place to another. Although small town Main Streets also displayed great similarity from town to town, there was more opportunity for distinctive display. Merchants were more inclined to decorate their buildings, since retailing was more dependent upon architectural display for business promotion. The facades along Main Streets and around courthouse squares served to make towns seem distinctive. Locals took pride in "downtown" as the ceremonial heart of the community. Although Main Street was owned by businessmen, it seemed to belong to everyone. Although the values of business ruled Main Street's creation, a larger sense of community aspiration prevailed. Small towners easily thought of Main Street in comparing their towns with other places. Visitors were shown the street with pride.

Three

Small-Town Society in the Railroad Era

Well, I'd better show you how our town lies. Up here—is Main Street. Way back there is the railway station; tracks go that way. Polish Town's across the tracks and some Cannuck families. Over there is the Congregational Church; across the street's the Presbyterian.
Thornton Wilder, *Our Town*

A small town was more than a place of business; it was home to the people who lived there. A town might be oriented commercially to Main Street and the railroad, but most of its area was given to residential use. Houses lined most streets, with schools and churches interspersed. Traditional town life involved small, inwardly focused populations occupying limited spaces. Accordingly, neighboring was intensive and highly personalized. Small-town society was easily stereotyped, and those stereotypes were easily symbolized in landscape. Landscape symbolization reinforced many conventional wisdoms about small towns as places to live.

The Grid

The street grid served as the base upon which most towns grew. Here was a laborsaving device without equal, for developers could plan towns from a distance with little exact knowledge of town sites.[1] Lots within the grid could be easily surveyed and conveniently numbered for quick sale. Thus the grid symbolized simplicity and efficiency in town building. It also symbolized an ordered environment. It was a classic American form much taken for granted in its widespread replication across the United States.

A town divided into uniform lots seemed more democratic and perhaps more intrinsically American, for land spelled equal opportunity when packaged as a commodity accessible to and affordable by many. Noel Houston writes of El Reno, the boom town in *The Great Promise*: "The uneasy decision, the uprooting, the arduous journey, all those were behind now; before them the final act, the actual possession of a parcel of earth where the dream could at last materialize. In the mind of every man and woman was the exquisite picture of the perfect home, the perfect yard, the perfect street running before it.''[2] The grid of a new town spelled opportunity.

A town's lots were usually large enough to accommodate a house, a vegetable garden, a barn or stable, and other buildings. Since tax assessments were based on front footage in most places, it was better for property owners to have long, narrow lots.[3] In the established towns, like Boulder, Colorado, street grids could be easily extended to accommodate growth. In Boulder the courthouse tower and adjacent business buildings rose above the canopy of trees to define the center of town; but at the town's periphery the grid of streets, devoid of trees, was clearly etched in the foothills of the Front Range.

View of Boulder, Colorado (circa 1910). The grid of streets upon which Boulder grew was most evident at the edge of town, where blocks were not yet obscured by trees.

While the grid street plan was functional, it also introduced a high order of monotony into small-town landscapes. Vistas along streets stretched to the horizon. Little terminated a view save the overhang of trees, and farm fields in the distance. In the Midwest and West, a grid of rural roads, oriented to the township and range survey system, repeated the grid on a larger scale. W. R. Wolfe writes of Puget Sound towns: ''The separate lot, sometimes built on, sometimes vacant, has produced a random punctuation of open space and a sense of disorganization. Many street scenes are endless; visual stops being furnished where the topography precluded the actual extension of section line or its parallel streets. Because of this . . . forced geometry, there are few elements of surprise.''[4]

A small town could be seen in its entirety from a nearby hill, the courthouse tower, or some other vantage point. It could be easily conceptualized—the grid of streets with or without concealing foliage contrasting with surrounding open country. The grid was like a checkerboard upon which a game was arranged. Often the courthouse was visible from all parts of the town, its tower lit at night by electric lights to remind residents of their commonality as a community. Many courthouse towers featured clocks and even time balls which, when lowered on tall poles, marked the correct time at noon. Tower and grid complemented one another—order in the horizontal dimension with order in the vertical.

A view of Main Street and adjacent business streets usually disclosed an orderly blending of residential and commercial buildings, as in Williston, North Dakota. As Booth Tarkington wrote, at some point "the mart gave way to the home."[5] Sometimes churches aided in the transition. A town's better residential properties were often located on the end of Main Street away from the railroad, but within easy walking distance of downtown stores. Here was a logical location for churches and other institutions subsidized by the more affluent residents. Not only were churches part of Main Street's architectural display, but they also served to buffer gentry houses from nearby businesses. Otherwise, the direct juxtaposition of residential and commercial land uses typified business district peripheries. Workshop, store, and home coexisted in a small, but ordered, transition zone.

View of Williston, North Dakota (1909). Many of the major elements which typified small-town landscapes are visible in this photograph. The business district blends with surrounding residential space. Grain elevators loom in the distance, marking the line of the railroad. A hotel, bank, and other distinctive landmarks are apparent in the business district by the size and silhouette of structure.

Residential Streets

In the century's early years, few streets beyond a town's business district were paved. Minor streets were weed choked, with the grooves of wagon and carriage wheels defining their centers. The better-travelled streets were periodically smoothed by horse-drawn road graders; sprinkler wagons dampened down the dust of summer. Residential streets were typically tree lined, especially in New England where village improvement societies used systematic tree planting to beautify the landscape.[6] Such was the case in Charlestown, New Hampshire, where rows of elm trees matured along the town's thoroughfares.

Street scene in Charlestown, New Hampshire (1916). The New England town was stereotyped for its tree-lined streets, which often radiated from a village green. Nearby was Main Street, the railroad, and usually a mill or factory. New England towns represented a significant regional variation on the American small-town theme.

The use of portland cement for sidewalk construction vastly upgraded the pedestrian-oriented town. The summer months resounded with the noise of cement mixers, as construction crews moved from street to street laying ribbons of concrete. Streets were paved with brick in the early years of the century although concrete was often used for curbing. Paved residential streets were usually narrow, but capable of accommodating horse-drawn traffic. Brick streets held a special charm. The sounds of horses' hooves and the narrow wagon and carriage wheels on the brick were distinctive. Brick streets glistened in the rain to reflect the glare of streetlights.

Many towns named their streets systematically. Streets might be num-

Sidewalk construction in Camden, Michigan (circa 1910). Towns had been built to walk through. The walk to work, school, or store as well as the leisurely stroll brought people into close contact with their habitat. The automobile later buffered people from their environment by enclosing them in a shell and moving them quickly down the street in a hurried, restless manner.

An improved residential street in Sullivan, Illinois (circa 1920). The popularity of the bicycle helped stimulate street improvements before the automobile. Brick streets predominated in the first two decades of the twentieth century, and portland cement and asphalt streets thereafter.

bered (First, Second, Third), named after the presidents (Washington, Adams, Jefferson), or named after trees (Chestnut, Elm, Willow). Homer Croy writes of fictional "Junction City, Missouri" and its "tree-lined streets—as straight and as regular as a checkerboard. . . . East and West the presidential streets ran, while the north-and-south streets enjoyed the names of trees. Thus there were Ash, Sycamore, Birch, Poplar, Pine, Mulberry, Vine, and so through the forestry catalogue."[7] Although streets might be named, they were not always marked. A look at a map or an abstract was often necessary to know what a street was rightfully called. Houses were better known than streets, and directions were given relative to where people lived. Introduction of house-to-house mail delivery forced small towns to erect street signs following post office regulations.

Power and telephone poles came to dominate streetscapes in the early decades of the twentieth century. Trees were cut down in many towns to accommodate the wires. Systematic tree planting along street margins ceased in many places, and shade trees were restricted to private yards. The cathedral-like effect of arching elms so brilliantly achieved in New England was no longer valued. Not until the 1920s did power companies emphasize the placement of poles along easements to the rear of houses. Residential streets came to reflect the utilitarian values of the power companies in many towns.

Downed wires in Homer, Illinois (1912). The power and telephone lines which had accumulated along small-town streets were quickly taken for granted. But when ice or wind storms brought the lines down, out came the photographers—both commercial and amateur—to record the spectacle.

The Gentry

A town's wealthier families set the tone in fashionable housing. The banker, the successful merchant, and the factory owner housed their families in limited luxury. A large house with a large lawn symbolized the good life in Booth Tarkington's *The Conquest of Canaan*: "It was a big, smooth-stone house, product of the Seventies, frowning under an outrageously insistent mansard, capped by a cupola, and staring out of long windows overtopped with ornamental slabs. Two cast-iron deer, painted death-gray, turns by the same mould, stood on opposite sides of the front walk." Big houses symbolized the assertion of power. Tarkington continues: "It was a hideous house, important-looking, cold, yet harshly aggressive, a house whose exterior provoked a shuddering guess of brass lambrequins and plush fringes within; a solid house, obviously—nay, blatantly—the residence of the principal citizen, whom it had grown to resemble . . . and it sat in the middle of its flat acre . . . like a rich, fat man enraged and sitting straight up in bed to swear."[8]

Gentry houses needed not only to be big, but stylish as well. Noel Houston depicts Sawyer Tyndall, his heroine in *The Great Promise*, planning her house with Mr. Collins, an architect:

> They poured through catalogues, sample floor plans, and pictures of houses which he brought, and though they readily came to an agreement on the general plan of the interior, none of the pictures showed just the exterior effect she wanted. "There!" she would exclaim, pointing to a mid-Victorian house dripping with milled gewgawry, "that's almost it—but it's not fancy enough. It's got to be fancy . . . it must be the kind of house that when people drive by and look at it, they won't just say, well, there's a house where somebody lives. It must excite their admiration—they must say, that beautiful structure is the residence of the famous Sawyer Tyndall—how coveted is an invitation to enter that elegant front door!"[9]

Not only did the gentry own the most impressive houses, but they bought and drove the first automobiles, as they had owned and driven the fanciest carriages. Part of the gentry's mystique sprang from their ability to afford the latest fads and fashions. W. L. White writes of the Browne family:

> The Brownes always did and had things first. They had the largest cut-glass punch bowl and the most gold-banded china and solid silver table-ware. The big Browne house stood on the best corner of Federal Street, Athena's oldest and finest residential thoroughfare. The granite shaft over old Grandpa Browne's grave was the tallest in

Athena Cemetery. The Brownes had had the first automobile (a Stanley Steamer), the first trip to Europe . . . and the first fifteen-by-eighteen oriental rug. They had the first radio . . . and were the first prominent Athena family to remove the iron deer from the front lawn.[10]

The residence of a gentry family at Homer, Illinois (circa 1915). The family's prized possessions included the new house and the automobile—both displayed for the photographer. The family itself is almost incidental to the photograph.

The gentry of most small towns lagged behind their big city counterparts. The dark colors, heavy furniture, and seemingly insatiable demand for clutter which characterized the Victorian era lasted longer in the small-town setting.

Home was a female preserve. Taste in interior furnishing and lawn and garden decoration was dictated by the women's magazines of the period. May Watts describes the changes in a hypothetical gentry household tended by an indulgent homemaker:

In the living room she arranged marigolds, or sunflowers, in a bean pot on the monk's cloth runner on the new black mission table that had replaced the golden oak. It stood beside the blue plush over-stuffed chair under the Maxfield Parrish picture with the very-blue sky, that had replaced the Rheims Cathedral. ("The Song of the Lark" had been replaced by a picture of "Old Ironsides," and the crayon portraits by Whistler's "Mother.")[11]

A small town's gentry was interrelated through business associations and, more importantly, through cultivated friendships reinforced by

A front parlor in Mabel, Minnesota (1907). Home was a female place. House decoration typically expressed female interests and inclinations, rather than male. The home was a place of limited luxury for wives and daughters of gentry families who could afford large houses and the "help" to keep them serviced.

"desirable marriages." Every town had an inner circle whose personal interests were so tightly interwoven with those of the community at large that one could not determine where self-interest ended and public spirit began.[12] The small-town gentry rarely acknowledged their privileges even in the face of extravagant expenditures on houses, motorcars, and other luxuries. In James West's "Plainville," a small Missouri town, the few gentry families had traditionally considered themselves "plain," "average," and "not outstanding."[13] They refused to acknowledge clear class differences, except to differentiate "rich" from "poor" or an "idle class" from a "working class." These beliefs were held generally throughout the community: "This is one place where ever'body is equal. You don't find no classes here."[14] West, nonetheless, diagrams an elaborate social hierarchy with an "upper crust." "Good, honest, self-respecting, average, everyday working people"; "good, lower class people"; and a "lower element," including "people who live like animals," made up the rest of "Plainville's" traditional social hierarchy.[15]

Social distinctions in the typical town reflected the way one's family lived (location of residence and type of dwelling), income and material possessions, participation in community affairs, family background, and individual reputation or prestige. Lewis Atherton observes: "A small inner group of people based on varying combinations of wealth, length of residence, occupation, and breeding stood at the top. God-fearing, middle class people devoted to church and lodge formed still another layer. And

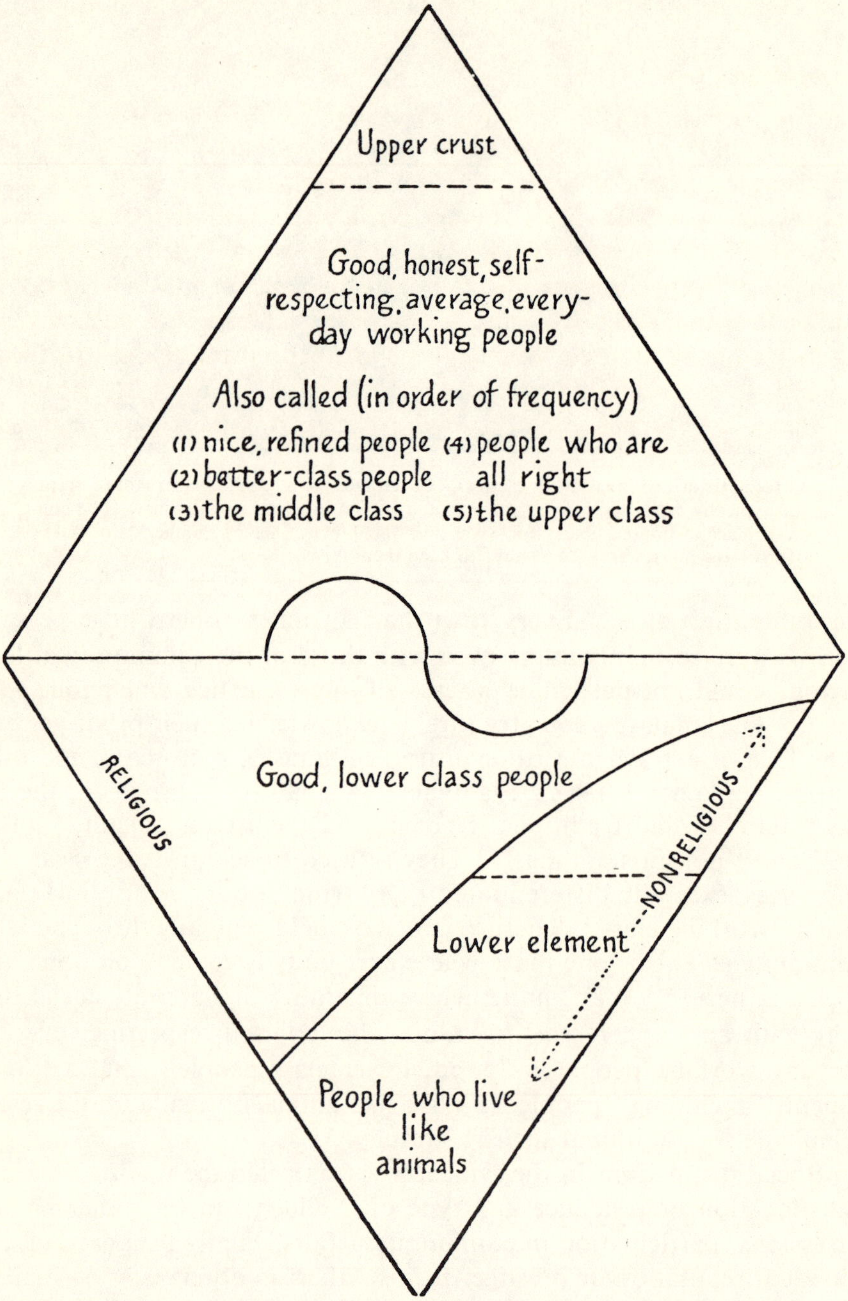

Upper crust

Good, honest, self-
respecting, average, everyday working people

Also called (in order of frequency)
(1) nice, refined people (4) people who are
(2) better-class people   all right
(3) the middle class   (5) the upper class

RELIGIOUS

Good, lower class people

NON RELIGIOUS

Lower element

People who live
like
animals

Social stratification traditional to James West's "Plainville." Source: James West, *Plainville, U.S.A.* (New York: Columbia University Press, 1946), p. 116.

always a lower class of common laborers, generally indifferent to dominant ideals, could be distinguished.'' Atherton also notes that these divisions were not discussed openly: "Ideals of a classless society and social purity ranked too high in the small town code to permit open doubts.''[16]

The Middle Class

The middle class formed the backbone of small-town society. The shopkeepers and the more successful artisans made the town run as the owners and operators of its smaller businesses. This was often a highly transient population which took risks, as often as not failed, and frequently moved on to brighter prospects elsewhere. Sinclair Lewis writes: "The Gopher Prairie jeweler sells out, for no discernable reason, and moves on to Alberta or the State of Washington, to a shop precisely like his former one, in a town precisely like the one he has left.'' Lewis also notes: "A man becomes a farmer, grocer, town policeman, garageman, restaurant-owner, postmaster, insurance-agent, and farmer all over again, and the community more or less patiently suffers from his lack of knowledge in each of his experiments.''[17] Many small-town entrepreneurs dabbled in a range of enterprise. Where the demand for any one service or product was limited, the small-town businessman became a jack-of-all-trades offering a range of services and products to make a living.

The middle class lived comfortably, but spent money on luxuries with great care. Compared to the gentry they had less time for leisure. Life focused on the home, the business, the church, and usually a fraternal organization. The houses of the middle class were scattered, with perhaps one or two streets dominated by more pretentious residences. There, in proximity to the town's few gentry families, a middle-class family might seek to display pretended affluence. Few houses possessed architectural styling. Most were constructed by local carpenters from standardized plan books, so a given house plan was often replicated throughout a town. On streets built by a single developer, houses might look very much alike except for minor details of porch decoration, window arrangement, or color. Such was the case on Oak Street in Buckley, Illinois.

Rose Wilder Lane describes the typical small-town home of the Midwest. Houses were covered with clapboards, and painted white or yellow with contrasting colors outlining their edges and framing windows and doors.

> The houses had no more architecture than boxes. Usually a gable faced the street, displaying in its windows white machine-lace curtains looped back on either side of the many small panes. Between these curtains the glass shone dark as deep water. Dusk filled that room; it was the parlor. . . . There would be a center-table decked with a

crocheted doily, a parlor lamp, and such ornaments as the family possessed. If it owned a book, the book lay here in state. The table's legs supported, a few inches above the carpet, a shelf as large as its top, and on the shelf there might be . . . a stereopticon [stereoscope] with its box of twin pictures, Niagara Falls, the Capitol at Washington, Views of the Chicago World's Fair, to be looked at through the hooded lenses. But stereopticons were no longer fashionable. What-nots, too, had gone out of style. A few parlors could boast a parlor organ, its high top adorned with scroll-saw work, inset mirrors, and small shelves displaying family photographs.[18]

Oak St looking North, Buckley, Ill.

47410.

Residential street in Buckley, Illinois. The middle class valued security and respectability in modest houses set on landscaped lawns along tree-lined streets, as pictured.

Houses looked pretty much alike, for the environment of the middle class was highly standardized. Lane continues:

> These little houses, all created to serve the need of shelter as cheaply as possible, resembled each other as sisters do. There was charm in the simplicity, though no one saw it. They were candid and innocent, and poverty kept them free of affectations. The utmost that individual taste could do was to vary the pattern of scroll-saw work along their eaves and to paint them a whiter white or a brighter yellow than their neighbors.[19]

At the turn of the century the typical middle-class house was lit by kerosene. Drinking water was obtained from domestic wells or private cisterns, except in the relatively few towns with water systems. The privy was attached to the woodshed out back.[20] After 1900 more and more houses were equipped with modern plumbing and central heating. This trend varied from region to region and with town size. For example, in "Plainville," a town of sixty-five houses, as late as 1946 only three houses were "completely modern."[21] A later study in 1961 revealed the "inside toilet" to be universally accepted by "Plainvillers," but still not universally installed, especially in the houses of low-income families.[22] Lacking bathrooms, people bathed infrequently. The stated ideal in "Plainville" had long been "a bath once a week."[23] Increased social status attached to those who had running water, indoor toilets, bathrooms, and central heat.

Most families sought to upgrade their living conditions. Many moved their residence frequently, especially if they were renters. New houses were in constant demand—houses with central heating, sound plumbing, and electrical wiring capable of handling the host of household appliances becoming available on the consumer market. Most people turned to standard plan books and many purchased prefabricated houses out of catalogues, with the materials delivered to and then assembled by a local contractor. After World War I the more style-conscious among the middle class built bungalows, especially if they lived in California or in Florida. Aspiring families also chose "Georgian," "Dutch Colonial," and "Cape Cod Cottages," among other revival styles. New houses filled many of the vacant lots left undeveloped during past building spurts. New and old houses mingled on the grid of streets.

A bungalow in Davista, Florida (1918). Many of the new styles of housing introduced into small towns after the turn of the century reflected big-city values. Bungalows spread from such centers as Los Angeles and Chicago. Many of the new homes were manufactured at distant factories to be assembled by local builders.

Low-Income People

A small town's poorer families lived in varied housing, from the hand-me-down older houses vacated by the more affluent, to small cottages built for them on speculation. The workingman's cross-plan house was very popular before World War I. Relatively few of the poorer families owned their own houses; most were renters. The typical house included a living room or "sitting room," a kitchen, and several bedrooms. In "Plainville," "the living room stove, or heater is the center of the family's leisure in winter—the best chairs are set around it. The walls are papered in floral patterns from Montgomery Ward or the drug or hardware store. They are further decorated with family 'enlargements' (especially of children or the dead), pretty advertising calendars, perhaps a magazine cover or two, and a few other momentoes."[24]

A cross-plan house, town unknown (circa 1920). Little effort has been expended on landscaping the property shown here. Less affluent families had little money for yard decoration and, if the husband was steadily employed, little time. The children's automobile adds a touch of luxury to an otherwise modest situation.

Generally, such families expended little money on the decoration or care of their yards. Most of "Plainville's" front yards contained one or two shade trees and some flowers—usually roses, hollyhocks, and smaller varieties grown in symmetrical flower beds bordered with stones, tin cans, bottles, bricks, or old rubber tires; or made of discarded wheels of corn planters, wagons, and other farm implements.[25] The backyards were totally functional, usually without landscaping. They were fenced with well-trodden paths leading from the back or side door to the privy, barn, and other outbuildings. The garden was located either directly behind the

Enjoying the back yard, town unknown (circa 1920). Backyards in both middle- and working-class neighborhoods tended to be utilitarian in the extreme. A storage shed, a privy, a chicken coop, several garden plots, fruit trees, and a clothesline are visible in this snapshot taken with a hand-held camera.

house, or to one side in order to accommodate a chicken yard or other feature. Cows as well as horses might be stabled in the barn, at least in the early decades of the century.

Rarely were backyards neatly kept, as Sinclair Lewis establishes for "Gopher Prairie." All winter residents had thrown garbage out their back doors, to be cleaned up in the spring. The first thaw "disclosed heaps of ashes, dog-bones, torn bedding, clotted paint cans, all half covered by icy pools which filled the hollows of the yards. The refuse had stained the water to vile colors of waste—thin red, sour yellow, streaky brown"[26] More than one observer found the clutter of backyards unsightly. Harlan Douglass, champion of small-town reform, complained of "unkept premises, of barns, poultry yards, manure heaps, wood piles, and nondescript outbuildings which outnumbered the dwellings." He calculated seven outbuildings to the typical small-town yard.[27]

The families of unskilled laborers who hired out by the day or week, or who worked for indefinite periods in mill or mine, lived at or near the poverty level. Small towns were filled with retired farmers who, having

57

been tenants or sharecroppers, were forced to leave the land in old age. Until the Depression of the 1930s, welfare in the small town was generally a private matter. Church women quietly surveyed the needs of destitute families and arranged for clothing, food, and jobs.

The Wrong Side of the Tracks

Harlan Douglass writes: "Most of the small towns of America are bisected by a railroad along which much of the ugliness concentrates, and which frequently divides the town socially as well as geographically. On the other side of the tracks are the poorer homes, the muddier streets, and the fewer sidewalks."[28] Rose Wilder Lane observes: "The railroad's raw embankment limited the region where nice people lived. . . . 'South of the tracks' was inevitably a limbo of shiftless ne'er-do-wells, section hands, men who drank and wives who took in washing, their children who mustn't be played with. Nice people lived north of the tracks."[29]

A town's minority people usually lived beyond the tracks. J. B. Jackson writes of towns in the American Southwest:

Cross Third Street and Second Street and Railroad Street; the buildings are shabby. . . . The surface of the streets is broken and full of dusty holes; there are overhead lines and half the trees are dying. Instead of neat white houses . . . there are close packed rows of frame tenements and duplexes . . . an occasional vacant lot, garages black with grease, corner groceries with screen doors, lodging houses. Here is where the local minority lives—Negroes or Spanish Americans or Indians or unassimilated Hillbillies along with idle old men and drifters vaguely looking for a harvesting or construction job. The section merges into a wasteland of rusting tracks, cinders, floodplain.[30]

In New England the minority community might be Italian, French Canadian, or possibly Polish. Companies sometimes built houses adjacent to the mills to accommodate these families. Seldom did the "foreign" element mingle with "native" Americans in the early years of an ethnic community: "Americans did not mix with oddities from Europe and so on. Foreigners were just labor."[31] In the Midwest the minority community might be German, Finnish, Swedish, or Norwegian. In California it might be Chinese, Japanese, or Filipino.

An extensive lore of fact, legend, and myth was connected with each of a town's minorities. Sociologist August Hollinghead writes of "Elmtown":

The Irish are supposed to be Catholics, Democrats, "hell raisers," fighters, "boozers," cheap politicians, troublemakers, and philanderers. The Germans are good, thrifty people, hard workers, money makers, a good element, some of the finest people. The Norwegians are characterized as clannish, cold sexually (but "a lot of the girls go wrong"), disinterested in education, religious ("religious as hell"), a good thrifty sort, hard workers, good citizens.[32]

In the South, blacks constituted the effective minority although in many towns whites were the actual minority in population terms. Hamilton Basso describes "Macedon's" black district—called "Niggertown" by whites, but known among the blacks as "High Rent":

> It was here that the more submerged life of the town, like a river beneath a river, went on—fish frys, steak roasts, beer parties, wakes, razorings, bi-weekly services in the Bethel A Colored Baptist Church. Poverty ran through the section like a plague, hunger was a frequent visitor or permanent boarder in almost every house, but the inhabitants of High Rent, merging a simple philosophy with the terrible patience of the poor, complained but little and trusted in the humanity of a singularly inhumane and white-faced God for eventual succor and release.[33]

Many of a town's misfits lived beyond the tracks. There was the town half-wit who was sent constantly on foolish errands by one practical joker or another—to the hardware store for a left-handed monkeywrench, or to

One of the more eccentric citizens of Homer, Illinois (1911). The traditional small town functioned much like an extended family to tolerate and protect eccentric personalities.

the print shop to see the type lice.[34] There lived the lonely people who let high hedges grow about yards, and left their houses unpainted with the porches rotting away. Every town had its eccentric citizens who added variety, if not color, to the community.

Neighboring

Neighboring was intensified in the small town early in the twentieth century. A small population occupied a limited space containing relatively few settings for socializing. Before the widespread use of automobiles, a town's residents were largely confined to interacting with one another. One constantly met the same people in the same places within the ebb and flow of daily, weekly, and seasonal cycles of activity. Socializing was frequent and personalized. People knew of one another through the constant gossip of frequent encounters.

Many spaces or places in the small town were specially structured to facilitate gossip and other forms of interaction. Most houses had front porches where people gathered in warm weather to view the sidewalk and to strike up conversations with neighbors passing by. Sometimes a yard became an extension of the porch with yard swings, lawn games, and other devices intended to promote socializing. R. L. Duffus remembers the porches of Waterbury, Vermont. While the women rocked, the men sat with their feet propped up on the porch rails. "You could count the holes in the bottoms of the shoes of half of Waterbury's grown-up males by strolling along the two or three principal streets on a late July Sunday."[35] Porch life was an important diversion from work, and furnishing the porch was done with care in gentry families. Potted plants were put out and vines trained to grow on porch columns. Goldfish in bowls and birds in cages added to the decor.[36]

Along Main Street and in the courthouse square, men habitually gathered to "sit, spit, smoke, chew, chat, and whittle together." In "Plainville," the male loafing group, while not rigidly organized, had long involved a central nucleus of membership. They were variously called the "old men," the "club," the "storytellers," the "real loafers here," or sometimes the "spit and whittle (or argue) club." The "club" sat throughout the summer on iron benches under a shade tree in one corner of the courthouse lawn. In bad weather and in the winter they moved into the stores. Only one or two stores lacked benches or chairs to accommodate gossipers.[37]

> The iron benches control a view of the street and everyone who enters it from any direction. The old men daily gather up all the threads of current events and gossip. They laugh, satirize, complain, approve,

60

A house equipped for neighboring, town unknown (circa 1905). The front porch was a place for spontaneous interaction with those passing by on the sidewalk. Informality reigned. The most trusted social relationships were those born of casual encounters frequently repeated.

Courting in a lawn swing, town unknown (circa 1910). In more affluent homes the front lawn was often an extension of the porch. Swings, chairs, and lawn games supported the neighboring process.

and disapprove. But their attitudes are more tolerant than is assumed by the women and girls who on each trip down the street have to pass by the old men, endure their scrutiny, and "wonder what they're saying now."[38]

The women of "Plainville" had their own places for gossip downtown. Women spoke of the notions store as "a place where ladies gather."[39] If a man entered the store, the conversation ceased and all eyes regarded him. The proprietress asked, "Did you want something?" To the men, these women were the "old women," the "widows," the "gossips," the "old gossips," the "busybodies," and the "snoops." Men viewed the notions store as "a clearinghouse for exchanging and garbling all news, especially scandal and any other news discreditable to individual reputations."[40]

News spread rapidly throughout a small town's acquaintance network. Sociologist Albert Blumenthal reports in *Small-Town Stuff*: "With such community of interest, and a general desire to tell the other fellow the latest news, it is not surprising that an exceptionally live bit of news, such as the death of a prominent citizen, attains almost complete circulation in the community in about two hours."[41] In "Mineville," a town of some fifteen hundred people on which Blumenthal's case study focused, the average adult listed nearly one-quarter of the population as speaking acquaintances. "By sight, name, or reputation he is aware of the presence of approximately nine-tenths of the adult persons, and seven-tenths of the children and youth."[42]

Neighboring followed prescribed patterns. James West describes "Plainville's" traditional code of conduct:

> Social discrimination may result in very extraordinary neighboring situations—a man may "neighbor" with another man, when the wife of one "would not neighbor" or "could not neighbor" with the other wife. Their small children may play together freely, running in and out of both homes and fed between meals by both mothers, while the post-adolescent girls of the "better family" are unable to "speak friendly in town" to the big boys of the other family. Meanwhile, perhaps, the larger boys in both families can hunt and "run around" together, and even "stay all night with each other." . . . It is astounding how complex the ritual and taboos on human intercourse can become even . . . where people like to say "we are just one plain old average, everyday, working class of people here."[43]

Intensive neighboring bred conformity. People mouthed the common truths, they conformed to expected norms in their behavior. Small-town humor was often little more than ridicule of those who could not or would not conform. Willa Cather writes in *My Antonia* of a small-town America made impotent by conformity.[44] She saw the frontier humor of the towns-people as a mechanism to promote conformity, agreeing with Anthony Hilfer that it was . . . "directed against all pretensions beyond the practical and the materialistic, against any expression of the inner life."[45] Cather writes:

> On starlight nights I used to pace up and down those long cold streets, scowling at the little sleeping houses on either side, with their storm windows and covered back porches. . . . The life that went on in them seemed to me made up of evasions and negations; shifts to save cooking, to save washing, and cleaning, devices to propitiate the tongue of gossip. This guarded mode of existence was like living under a tyranny. People's speech, their voices, their very glances, became repressed. Every individual taste, every natural appetite, was bridled by caution. The people asleep in those houses, I thought, tried to live like the mice in their own kitchens; to make no noise, to leave no trace, to slip over the surface of things in the dark."[46]

According to this thinking, creative people didn't last long in the small town. They either conformed or escaped to the city.

Conformity was also the central theme of Sinclair Lewis's *Main Street*. What really bothered Carol Kennicott was not the ugliness of "Gopher Prairie" or its injustice, as Hilfer puts it, but, "the soul destroying intellectual conformity that leads to a pervasive and inescapable dullness."[47] The machine is the dominant metaphor in *Main Street*. The townspeople sit "in rocking chairs . . . listening to mechanical music, saying mechanical things . . . when a standard prejudice is mouthed, the townspeople nod solemnly and in tune, like a shop window of flexible toys, comic mandarins, and judges and ducks and clowns, set quivering by a breeze from the open door."[48]

The pressure to conform often hindered change and slowed progress. Intensive neighboring bred an inherent conservatism. Newell Sims writes of "Aton" and the effect of public opinion on the issue of licensing taverns. Voters in large numbers signed petitions against licensing, for not to do so publicly meant general censure. Nonetheless, when an election was held where people could vote as they pleased in private, the taverns were easily voted in.[49] Small-town animosities could run deep. Blumenthal writes of "Mineville": "To no small extent action prejudicial or contrary to the wishes of an individual or group causes personal alignments on various sides of a question. And so by the unwillingness of the sponsors of progress to arouse personal antagonisms by vigorously asserting their stand, advance is often held in abeyance and made difficult.[50]

Intensive neighboring also had its positive side. The individual knew that he belonged to a community. He could clearly identify himself not only as a resident of a specific town, but as being a small-town person in general. Living in the small town carried with it a whole assortment of positive stereotypes—honesty, fair play, trustworthiness, helpfulness, sobriety, clean living.[51] Above all, small towns were seen as friendly places where neighboring, despite its negative connotations, was highly personalized and, at least superficially, pleasant.

Few institutions promoted a small town's image as a friendly place more than the town newspaper. Local newspapers enhanced the sense of community by emphasizing the activities of local people, irrespective of how commonplace those activities might be. Reporters met the trains to detail the comings and goings of local residents. Births, baptisms, parties, meetings, and funerals were all dutifully reported. James West writes that subscribers to the "Plainville" weekly generally read the neighborhood news first, in order to examine the extent of the reporting of what they had already heard on the party line, over fences, in town, and from school-children.[52] The small-town newspaper dignified the lives of common people by assuming that their activities were important.[53] Newspapers emphasized the positive. They rarely reported local arrests, shotgun weddings, mortgage foreclosures, lawsuits, bitter exchanges in public meetings, suicides, or any other unpleasant happening.[54] As newspapers focused on the sunny side of life, the community facade took on a warm and pleasing glow.

Conclusion

The grid of streets, although modified from place to place to fit local conditions, represented an American small-town universal. The grid served the needs of land development and speculation, but its popularity was rooted in a broader ethic. It imposed a sense of class equality—lots of equal size in a system of equal streets. Lots limited the size of houses except where several lots were brought together. No one street had a natural locational advantage, unless it was the better end of Main Street with its greater accessibility to business, and its greater visibility. Gentry houses clustered there; but elsewhere middle- and lower-income families were intermixed on the grid in housing of variable quality. Even on the "wrong side of the tracks," where ethnic minorities were usually located, the housing was of mixed quality although generally toward the lower end of the spectrum. The likelihood of living next door to someone substantially "richer" or "poorer" than oneself was high in the American small town in the early twentieth century. The idea of small-town social equality was encouraged by residential mixing. The diagram illustrates the mingling of gentry, middle-class, and workingmen's houses in a hypothetical small town of the railroad era.

Residential segregation did enhance ethnic and racial identities.

64

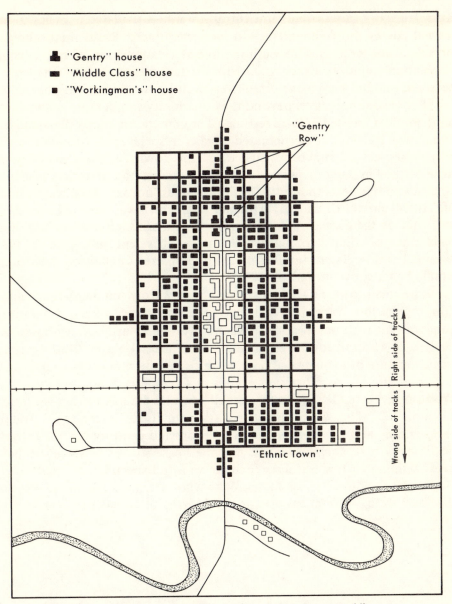

"Gentry" house

"Middle Class" house

"Workingman's" house

"Gentry Row"

Right side of tracks

Wrong side of tracks

"Ethnic Town"

A hypothetical small town: residential orientation before the automobile age.

"Ethnic Town" characterized the least affluent part of town, near the mill or mine. Ethnic and racial differences were rooted in occupational and income differences for the labor of minority people was usually unskilled and poorly paid. Minority communities sought isolation in small-town geography even when not ostracized by society at large. For the majority, social identity was derived less from residential location and more from the intensive and highly personalized ties of neighboring and friendship.

Knowledge of other people came through a well-articulated network of informal gossip and frequent face-to-face encounters. Residential segregation was not necessary to defining social relationships where a small population found itself restricted to a limited area. Behavior was highly personalized and people were relatively well known to one another.

People did not travel beyond the community frequently, so social interaction was focused in local settings. The climate for highly personalized interaction created and perpetuated a belief in social equality even though very strong class distinctions existed in most towns. If these distinctions were masked in daily socializing, they were almost obscured in landscape. On the grid of streets the gentry built the largest houses, but always under the critical gaze of those less fortunate: small-town ways exerted a leveling influence on the display of wealth. Poorer families aspired to wealth, and their close proximity to more affluent families lent substance to that dream. The mingling of families on the grid of streets enhanced the idea of equality as a conventional wisdom.

The small-town novel focused on the upwardly mobile, with the notion implicit in most novels that merit and persistence won out over inequality in the fortunes of a town. Such novels necessarily concentrated on the people who ran towns, especially as commercial places. Photography was a measure of affluence and ownership. Family snapshots emphasized the good life of comfort and stability. Commercial photography did likewise: postcards that painted a small-town landscape in negative terms did not sell. The visual image of the small town created through photography and novels was one of comfort and gentility for all. It took the objectivity of social scientists and their case studies to suggest otherwise. Although a few novelists focused on a full spectrum of small-town life, it was sociologists like James West who systematically identified the class and status differences obscured by myths of equality.

Four

Living in Small Towns before the Automobile

The village day went on. Everywhere the invisible ruled. The sign of the Angelus was given from the steeple, and the memorial to the moment—mystic and imperishable—beat in many hearts. The little shops were opened, and out came the humble symbols—cakes, fruits, fabrics. Awnings were lowered, watering-cans made cool the boards, anaemic little boys drew large maps across the windows. A faint odor of brown crust began to steal from the bakery.
Zona Gale, *Birth*

Life in the small town revolved in a series of cycles. Each day saw a round of activities—patterns of behavior focused on home, work, school, and recreation. Time was also organized on a weekly basis. Some assigned a special task to each day of the week; almost everyone took Sunday as a day of rest. Likewise the seasons had their separate personalities. Work was steady at some periods and slack at others, for the typical town was close to the cycles of planting and harvesting on nearby farms. Cycles affected individuals according to the role each person played in the community. Women tended to organize time differently than men, the young differently than the old. Growing up, getting started, living, and retiring in the small town each had its problems and its rewards of the moment. A town's grid of streets contained an ebb and flow of life.

The Daily Cycle

In the early years of the twentieth century, the day began at sunrise. People started earlier in the long days of summer, and later in the winter. The fire was lit in the kitchen stove and slowly the household came to life, each member to go variously into the community on his or her daily rounds. Wives stayed at home until late in the morning or until the afternoon, when grocery shopping or club meetings took them out. But husbands and older children left early, the men for work and the children for school.

Woman's work was in the home; except for unmarried females, few women worked outside the home early in the century. Thorton Wilder's "stage manager" in *Our Town* could easily stereotype the small town wife and mother. His audiences readily understood: "I don't have to point out to the women in my audience that those ladies they see before them, both these ladies cooked three meals a day;—one of 'em for twenty years, the other for forty,—and no summer vacation. They brought up two children a piece; washed; cleaned the house—and never a nervous breakdown. Never thought themselves hard used either!"[1] Zona Gale writes of small-town women who "prepare breakfasts, put up lunches, turn the attention to the garden, and all, so to speak, with the left hand; ready at any moment to enter upon the real business of life—to minister to the sick or bury the dead, or conduct a town meeting or a church supper or a birth. They have a kind of goddess-like competence, these women."[2]

Not everyone saw the small-town women as heroic. Sinclair Lewis's Carol Kennicott found "Gopher Prairie's" society of females stultifying. In *Main Street* the woman's club came to symbolize incompetence and

Home of the "Country Contributor" at Rockville, Indiana (1912). Daughter of a small-town newspaper editor, the "Country Contributor" wrote a regular column for the *Ladies Home Journal*, thus bringing a degree of national prominence to her community. The column stereotyped women as home-oriented helpmates preoccupied with raising children and tending house.

even ignorance in the guise of culture and community service.[3] H. L. Mencken took every opportunity to satirize small-town culture in *The American Mercury* magazine: "One of the most cultural programmes ever given by the woman's club was enjoyed by its members . . . Mrs. Eaves gave, in her own fluent way, a very instructive talk on 'How to Use the Victrola.'"[4] Women were generally portrayed as ineffectual beyond the home. This stereotype, rooted in small-town tradition, received wide circulation even in national women's magazines. Between 1905 and 1918, for example, the "Country Contributor" wrote regularly for the *Ladies Home Journal* from her home in Rockville, Indiana. The column was filled with observation and advice generally reflective of woman's role as housewife: "If you have some raw conditions facing you this March—an old house maybe with carpets showing their teeth, curtains draggled, furniture rundown, hen houses dilapidated, fences demoralized, and the problem of base living staring at you—you are facing the call to greatness."[5] Should a woman aspire to anything higher than running her home,

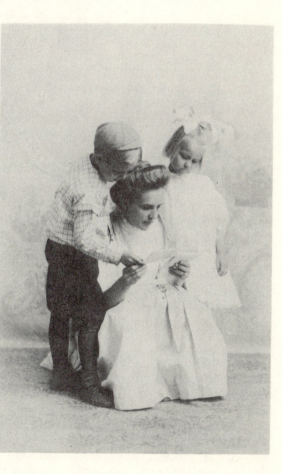

Portrait of a mother with her children taken at an Angola, Indiana, photographer's studio (1905). Portrait photography constituted the bulk of the commercial photographer's business in small towns. Postcards of local scenery were usually a sideline. Studios were equipped to simulate home settings to give women and children the appropriate background for the stereotyped images of family life.

Displaying hybrid corn in Newman, Illinois (1919). Main Street, as a place of business, was a male preserve. The commerce of most towns was rooted in agriculture as this photograph implies. Before World War I men rarely ventured downtown without a coat, and almost never without a hat.

and tending her husband and children? The stereotyped woman did not.

The man's work and, therefore, the man's world was away from home. His workplace was the store, the factory, the mine. Males dominated photographs of Main Street as, indeed, they dominated the street. Each morning the family's breadwinner walked or rode a bicycle to work. The more affluent relied on carriages. Much of a woman's pride, and indeed the family's status generally, derived from her husband's work and his place of work. By postcard from Minnesota's Messabi Range came the message: "Here is the engine Ed works on. He is near the X. This is taken down in the mine. That big bank is solid iron ore. We are well. Love Dora."

Home and workplace were the principle focal points of small-town life. As the typical town was primarily a trade center, most jobs were located on or near Main Street. Rose Wilder Lane observes:

There was a feeling that the center of town was masculine. Ladies went there, but with a certain circumspection. Usually they went in couples and a lady-like reserve was expressed in the propriety of their manner and in the care with which they held their skirts high enough to escape contamination from the sidewalk. . . . Ladies went uptown only for some definite purpose. They might enter the general store, the post office, the grocery store and the drug store, but they did not linger in these places, and on the streets they passed the livery-stable, the barber shop, the pool-room and above all the saloon with a manner so haughtily oblivious that it all but denied the existence of these places of doubtful virtue or all-too-certain vice.[6]

A Minnesota iron mine (1921). Factory, mill, and mine were male dominated. Men took pride in the machines they operated as symbols of strength and power. They took pride in the work they did as breadwinners in support of their families.

The shop owner moved between home and Main Street two or three times a day, his wife but a few times a week. His children visited Main Street every day after school.

On Main Street the daily cycle began about 6:00 A.M. when certain restaurants opened, to be followed by other businesses—especially those which emphasized the early morning trade as, for example, the ''Green Turtle Meat'' store in Key West, Florida. After the morning Angelus from the tower of the Catholic church or after the first factory whistle, more businesses opened as people began to fill the street. Ferdinand Reyher describes Ben Halper's arrival at his ''Sevillinois'' barbershop:

He got to the shop with the working day's beginning, and harkened to the street sounds, footfalls, drays, awnings coming down, so-and-so's door bang, and a screen door screeching, or somebody sweeping, the ring of Fahnestock's anvil in the distance on a particularly quiet morning, the lurching rumble of the road roller, the clop of the milk horse, the underlying vibrating of the linotype machine, the turning of the big coffee mill in Bammeyer's grocery store across the way that evoked a warm brown smell, or it might be winter and there was the rasping but pleasant sound of snow shovels.[7]

71

Store in Key West, Florida (1913). People were naturally drawn to the extraordinary in buildings and street scenes. This photograph was taken by a vacationer from Indiana who found the daily sale of turtle meat in Key West unusual.

Blumenthal writes of "Mineville": "Somewhat to the amusement of fellow-townsmen, even those who are notoriously idle rush toward their establishments in a most hurried walk as if an overwhelming amount of business awaits their arrival."[8] Zona Gale writes: "All down the little Main Street men came to work. They thought about the orders they must fill that day, the amounts due them; a train whistled, and they knew that it was ten minutes late."[9]

The post office felt the rhythms of the day. The "Mineville" postmaster bagged the evening's accumulation of letters from the one mailbox in front of the post office and met the morning train. After the train had arrived, the next major interest was expressed in the query: "Is the mail distributed yet?"[10] "In the cramped post office the contents of a lean bag were distributed by the old post-master; as slowly as if the mail were the mills of God; dusty, fly-specked little hole, where the state functioned so precisely as under hard wood and marble; and, in their tiny glass coffins, marked with worn red letters, were popped the missives of death, of life, of love, of unspeakable commonplace."[11] With the coming of the motor truck, mail delivery was pushed further into the day. Someone from practically every family in town, and from nearby farms, either walked or drove to the post office at mid-morning to check the mail.[12]

At noon the flow of schoolchildren through the downtown quickened the pace of life on Main Street. "A loose horse appears. She gallops in the brick walks and on the side-walk boards. Everybody who has oats comes running with a hatful of oats. She dodges down an alley. Her master comes running, the horse takes the bridle, and everybody turns indoors, secretly disappointed."[13] Businessmen joined the rush home for dinner to return as quickly again, for early afternoon was a busy time when most housewives came to do their shopping. But the peak of the day was reached about four o'clock when the confluence of children coming from the schools and men going to and from work added to the shopping and mail-getting group already present.[14] Slowly the typical afternoon slipped away and was gone, little of note seemingly ever accomplished. "A few women water the plants. Ministers go patiently about making expected calls and entering them in their little books. A load of hay comes creaking under the elms."[15]

At six o'clock the evening Angelus rang, or the roundhouse or brick-yard whistle blew. "All the tension of the day dissolves," writes Zona Gale of the fictional town of "Burage." "A new air permeates the village. It relaxes, expects. All Burage either goes home or welcomes home."[16] After supper the streets filled with people less hurried. Main Street became a leisure-time resort. Men excused themselves from supper tables to walk downtown to chat with friends. Women and girls were to be seen, but most of them did not tarry upon the streets: they tended to go directly to the theater, the ice-cream parlor, or a restaurant.[17] Others stayed home, catching up on the day's chores or relaxing. Sinclair Lewis's Carol Kennicot "rested at home. She listened to the village noises . . . sounds simple and charged with magic—dogs barking, chickens making a gurgling sound of content, children at play, a man beating a rug, wind in the cottonwood trees, a locust fiddling, a footstep on the walk, jaunty voices of Bea and a grocers boy in the kitchen, a clinking anvil, a piano—not too near."[18]

Hamilton Basso describes the closing down of "Macedon's" business district around the courthouse square:

> Still standing on the sidewalk . . . old Jim the Negro doorman counted the measured bells of time. Save for the yellow maw of the hotel entrance the blue flickering street lights that seemed a component of the shadows, the street was dark and deserted . . . even Mr. Roshefsky had locked the door of the Imperial Dry Goods Emporium and walked down the street in his greenish derby and musty black over coat, his head hunched in his shoulders like a crane at rest, wrapped in the enormous solitude of a single Jew in a totally Christian land. "One mo' hour," Jim stretched and yawned. . . . "One mo' hour and a man kin get some rest."[19]

The Weekly Cycle

After the housewife's morning round of chores was done, there came the week's routine. Rose Wilder Lane writes: "Only grave sickness or sudden calamity broke that proper routine: washing on Monday, ironing on Tuesday, mending on Wednesday, sewing on Thursday, extra cleaning on

Friday, baking on Saturday.''[20] Stores stayed open on Wednesday and Saturday nights in many towns, but only on Friday nights in other places. Similarly, businesses often closed one or more afternoons a week. Meetings of the county commissioners or the town council were held regularly each week as were lodge meetings—the Masons, the Oddfellows, the Knights of Pythias. So also did women's auxiliaries meet—the Rebeccas, the Eastern Star, the Pythian Sisters. Service clubs, such as the Rotary and Kiwanis, met regularly for dinner. The Boy Scouts and Christian Endeavor (or their equivalents) attracted their appropriate clientele one night a week. Payday at the factory or the mine made the saloons a little fuller. Rainy days were quite busy for the merchants, as farmers often used bad weather to catch up on accumulated shopping.[21]

Sunday was called a day of rest, but according to Rose Wilder Lane it was really ''the day on which the smooth bland surface of living became thicker than enamel.'' It was a day for dressing up, the day for church. Lane writes: ''We walked differently on Sundays, with greater propriety and stateliness. Greetings were more formal, more subdued, voices more meticulously polite. In church the rustling and stillness were alike pervaded with the knowledge that all was for the best. Propriety ruled the universe. God was in His Heaven, and we were in our Sunday clothes.'' Sunday was also a day for special ''fixings'' at dinner. ''Sunday afternoons had the mellowness of an over-ripe apple. In the winter the heater's

A family in Mendon, Michigan (1917). Amateur expertise with a camera imitated the studio poses created by the commercial photographers. Most family snapshot albums before World War I suggested that small-town people were forever dressed in Sunday finery.

warmth enveloped us. We sank into a lethargy of woolly underwear, of serge dresses and black broadcloth. In summer we sat on the shady front porch. . . . Parents nodded and roused to fan themselves with the folded church weekly and to crush a yawn.[22]

The Seasonal Cycle

The small town was close to nature's seasonal cycle. Open country was at hand, and the town itself had much of the country in it. Gardens produced most of the summer vegetables: "Through those first warm days [of spring] we watched the dandelions, lamb's quarter, dock and wild mustard growing large enough to pick for greens. Then from our gardens we got young onions, radishes, and lettuce leaves to be served with vinegar and sugar. Strawberries came in May; peas and new potatoes followed; then string beans, beets, turnips, carrots, sweet corn, tomatoes, and the full tide of summer's fruits."[23] To Sherwood Anderson, spring was the time of year when the country was felt most in a town. Spring brought a new aliveness: "more color in the windows of stores, spring term of court in country seat towns, a stir, an awakening, feel of earth invading the towns, smell of earth, new hope, warm spring rains, the vivid new green grass on lawns before the houses, the children looking forward to the end of the school year, to swimming in the town's pond or in the creek, to barefoot days."[24]

Summer was the best time of year for some. From Rockville, Indiana, the "Country Contributor" writes:

> Looking back over a half century it seems to me that life has been marked by a succession of summers. Nothing much ever happened in the wintertime. Winter in retrospect forms just one picture to me—simply keeping warm until things begin happening again. This is because I have lived in a rural place wherein the doings of Nature, the experiences of growing things, of domestic animals, fowls, have mingled happily with picnics, the camping excursions, the general outdoor atmosphere of the summertime.[25]

Summer was "a time of mosquitoes, of summer rains, of hot still weekdays on Main Street, no coal bills, greens from the garden, roasting ear time."[26] Summer was punctuated by Decoration Day, the Fourth of July, and Old Settlers Day.

Fall was a time for harvest. In the Midwest the grain elevators came alive. In the South the tobacco markets and cotton compresses were opened up. In Louisiana the sugar cutting began. "You see the children of the towns, white and black, each sucking away at a joint of cane."[27] Early autumn was also a time for fairs. County fairs brought the country and the town together for the celebration of rural life. Pavilions housed displays of farm commodities and household arts and crafts. Implement dealers demonstrated their wares. Politicians anticipated upcoming elections. Trotters and pacers kept the track and grandstand active.

Fair time in Texas, town unknown (circa 1920). Crowds mill along a midway where amusements mingled with agricultural displays. Fairs were held in late summer in the Northeast and Midwest, and later in the South. In the West fairs were often replaced by rodeos and jamborees. A fair was a deliberate celebration of the seasonal cycle.

Winter was a quiet time. For those who could afford it, winter was a time of escape by train to California or to Florida. For those left behind, it was a time to conserve energy in anticipation of the spring. Christmas brought subdued excitement little felt beyond the churches and the home. In the North towns were often snowbound, cut off from the outside world for days at a time. Few farmers came to town even in the best weather. Winter was a time for planned entertainments—lectures and shows at the opera house, motion pictures, church revival meetings, basketball games at the high-school gymnasium. The small town was essentially a "summer place." The great bulk of small-town photography was shot in warm weather. Winter pictures were almost always of unusual snow and ice scenes photographed after a big storm.

The town band highlighted special events especially in summer. A weekly concert from the bandstand in the park or courthouse square was a regular summer celebration: "The band represents the town on its gay days, when the fair comes, when there is a celebration, Fourth of July, any kind of jamboree, when every citizen becomes a boy again. . . . What is a town without a good band?"[28] A circus was better than a band. Every few

Coronet band in an undetermined Bloomingdale (circa 1905). There was a town named Bloomingdale in Georgia, Illinois, Indiana, Michigan, New Jersey, New York, Ohio, and Wisconsin. The repetition of small-town names from one state to another contributed to the notion that most small towns were very much alike.

Circus parade in Norfolk, Nebraska (1908). A circus parade was a special event. The dentist, Dr. Mittelstadt, whose office was located on the right, probably quit work for the day. Certainly the occupants of Brocadero's Saloon, located down the street, spilled onto the sidewalk to watch the spectacle. The circus promised unusual sights to break the tedium of everyday routines.

years a circus would arrive, pitch its tent at the edge of town, and stage a parade right down Main Street. A circus could make a small boy's summer. Indeed, a circus—even the smallest of carnivals—broke the monotony of small-town living for everyone. A summer could be remembered for nothing else but a circus.

The Life Cycle

To be born, grow up, live, and die in a given town was a pattern followed by relatively few Americans in the twentieth century. It was common for small-town youths to leave their communities for the assumed economic and social advantages of big-city living. A few emigrants might return to their "hometowns" late in life to retire, but by and large small towns were essentially incubators for big-city populations. A small town's population was usually heavy at both ends of its age spectrum—relatively more children and elderly persons than might otherwise have been expected. Young and old people did much to define the character of small towns. They were themselves icons of place.

Boyhood in the small town had the ring of magic about it when viewed from old age, especially after a lifetime spent in cities. Sherwood Anderson writes: "During all his life in the city, the small town of his boyhood has remained home to him. Every home in the town, faces of people seen on the street in his boyhood, have all remained sharply in his mind. How clearly he remembers the hill above the water-works pond, where he, with a troupe of other boys, went along a path beside a wheat field to the town swimming hole. He remembers the way the wind played in the wheat."[29] Lewis Atherton writes:

> Nostalgia for one's youthful kinship with the spirit of Tom Sawyer
> never departed from adults who grew up in . . . country towns. When
> Herbert Hoover later spoke of the swimming hole under the willows
> by the railroad bridge near his boyhood home in West Branch, Iowa,
> of trapping rabbits with box traps; of fishing with willow poles, and
> spitting on the bait to assure success, he plumbed the very heart out of
> the Midwest.[30]

Small-town boyhoods were remembered as vital preparations for successful lives. The historian Bruce Catton observes: "Our town was a tiny fragment of the American whole, sliced off for the microscope, showing in an enlarged form the inner characteristics of the larger society, and my boyhood in turn was a slice of the town, with its quaint fundamentals greatly magnified." Catton sees the small town and youth as synonomous. Youth cannot last. "Living in it is like waiting in a junction town for the morning limited. The junction may be interesting but some day you will have to leave it and you do not know where the limited will take you."[31]

Presumably, small-town adolescents realized their privileged status in time and place. David Barondess, Hamilton Basso's principal character in *Court House Square,* "closed his eyes, trying to impress the street on his memory. Some day he might need it for something—the sulfur color of the sun, the sentinel faces of the courthouse clock, the languid, blue-overalled movement of figures on the courthouse steps, the sheen on the pigeons' necks as they strolled the street in search of grain."[32] But home was never the same to adults who returned, especially after long absences. The images that had been ingrained on the mind were too vivid, too exaggerated. Marius Robinson returned to "Malice Landing" in Ohio, leaving behind his work in the city:

> He was mixed up. His uncle's house and garden had shrunk, and the very cherry tree on the knoll behind the back yard had grown smaller and more frail. The street had narrowed, and the Indian mound in the park huddled into itself until it was not much taller than Marius. The whole place was like a miniature of its earlier self carved out painstakingly and set under a glass bell, and Marius felt as if he were an artificial man walking through it all.[33]

Somehow girls never figured prominently in American literature as having had exciting small-town childhoods. Perhaps they were more restricted to home, more burdened with family chores, less inclined to wander at a distance in search of adventure real or imagined. Or perhaps grown-up girls have been less smitten by the bug of nostalgia to record in writing their exaggerated memories. Nevertheless, childhood in the small town was important to both boys and girls. The word *hometown* had deep meaning. Page Smith observes that the town was home, a kind of extended family.[34] "The town was made up like the family, of a number of individuals who lived for the most part, in a face-to-face relationship. . . . The town like the home became the symbol of a world of intimacy, warmth, acceptance, and security. Entangled as it was with the family, the town was searched and yearned for through the restless insecurity of urban, industrial America."[35]

The town gave the average child an extraordinary degree of freedom and security. One encountered a wide range of human activity and environment in a relatively small space. One's education was often vivid and immediate. William Allen White observes that there was little to teach a boy who had grown up "around the slaughter house and in the livery stable, who had roamed through romantic woods where the peripatetic strumpets made their camps, who had picked up his sex education from the Saxon words chalked on sidewalks and barns . . . and who had taken his Rabelaisian poetry from the walls of backhouses, and who had seen

79

saloons spew out their back door their indigestible drunkards, swarming with flies.''[36] Yet rarely were the unsavory things the essence of professed nostalgia. Even Sinclair Lewis saw his hometown in a romantic light. He wrote for the fiftieth anniversary edition of his high school's annual: ''I am quite certain that I could have been born and raised in no place in the world where I would have had more friendliness.'' He wrote of the ''fun he had had as a kid, swimming and fishing in Sauk Lake, or cruising its perilous depths on a raft . . . tramping out to the fairy lake for a picnic,'' and concluded: ''It was a good time, a good place, and a good preparation for life.''[37]

A family portrait from Shattuck, Oklahoma (1911). A photographer has been hired to picture a family reunited. The pose is formal, as is the dress.

The annual family reunion was a time when all generations came together to see and to be seen by people who might otherwise be known only through their pictures in family albums. Of course, reunions provided the material for more photographs, pictures which varied in style over time—from the very formal at the turn of the century when photography was relatively new, to the less formal later on. Families changed, and rapidly so between the two world wars. In the 1940s families were smaller than they had been, and more widely dispersed geographically. Fewer people attended the reunions which were held less frequently. But the pictures continued to be taken, with the old patriarch or matriarch given an honored place up front with the children. Center position was reserved for the more successful or more dominant family members whose good fortunes promised some degree of security for all. The people in the albums aged; old faces disappeared to be replaced by new ones.

A family portrait, town unknown (circa 1935). Amateur photographers were adequate to recording the reunions of the 1930s, so dependable had snapshot cameras become. Here the pose and dress are relatively informal.

Young marrieds from Shattuck, Oklahoma (1911). "Getting started" in a small town was not unusual, although most small towners by 1911 probably suspected that opportunities were greater in the cities.

Before the Depression people married young, often before they were well established financially. Witness Mr. and Mrs. David Donnikov. From Shattuck, Oklahoma, to Holyoke, Colorado, came this message on the back of their postcard picture: "Dear Friend Bessie. How are you. This is a picture of me and my wife. We wish you many happy birthdays to come. Your friend. David." With marriage came new responsibilities: for example, the need for bigger and more permanent housing. Above all, there was a need for job security. Marriage was a process of settling down, aided and sometimes abetted by tightly knit families and the always interested community.

Children were born, reached the toddler stage, and were off to school. James West writes of "Plainville's" youth: "His first day in school is a 'high point' to himself and to his mother, who 'always cries' when she sends him, dinner bucket in hand, down the road to the schoolhouse. Everybody jokes and brags on a 'first year scholar.'"[38]

"Old people" were those whose children had married and left home, and whose physical vigor had begun to decline. They were seen to be less

First day of school (circa 1900). This snapshot was reprinted on postcard paper and mailed to relatives and friends. It says much about the family's social status, and its position in the life cycle. The father, dressed as a laborer, lurks cautiously in the background. The house is probably rented, given the lack of repair to porch and shutters. But the family has aspirations: mother presumably owns a camera, and all of daughter's clothes are store-bought.

82

Civil War veterans at Earlville, Illinois (circa 1910). Nothing reminded Americans of the passage of time like the annual reunion of the Grand Army of the Republic or the Sons of the Confederacy. Each year fewer and fewer old-timers appeared with their ribbons and ancient flags.

alert; their opinions were no longer received with the respect once shown.[39] The elderly who could no longer stay by themselves lived with the families of sons or daughters, or in nursing homes. Nursing homes were more common after the Depression than before, for later families were smaller and less capable of tending incapacitated elders.

Once a year most towns celebrated their older citizens on "Old Settlers Day," or when the grand Army of the Republic or the Confederate Veterans held their reunions. Theodore Drieser describes Old Settlers Day at Columbia City, Indiana, in 1914. The streets were filled with people and wagons, and the square with tents. "Here were men and women so old and worn and bent and crumpled by the aging processes of life that they looked like the yellow leaves of the autumn. Nearly all the older ones, to add to their picturesqueness, wore bits of gold lettered cloth which stated clearly that they were old settlers."[40] Small towns cast glamour on those ancestors who "showing initiative and energy lacking in their descendants" had "carved out a whole new civilization in the wilderness."[41]

Leisure Time

The small-town resident was never far from the country. Madison, Indiana, for example, was surrounded by woods, hedgerows, and open fields in easy walking distance for every resident. Most small-town families had ready access to farm environments. Children were sent periodically to live with farm relatives, perhaps grandparents or aunts and uncles. Men

View of Madison, Indiana (circa 1910). Small towns could be glimpsed in a single view from a nearby hill. Set off from surrounding open spaces, towns like Madison were easily viewed as distinctive entities. Close proximity to fields, woods, and the river also engendered a closeness to nature or, at least, the opportunity for that closeness.

Farmstead near Fullerton, North Dakota (circa 1910). Most small towners took pride at being "urban" and many looked with disdain on farm families for their isolation. Nonetheless, most small towns were rooted in agricultural economy, and in various ways the farm scene was a part of small-town life.

and boys from town might help farm relatives with harvesting or planting when extra hands were needed. Work on a threshing crew meant hard work, but it also provided a change of pace. Wives and older girls drove out from town to help feed the threshing crews, or perhaps just to visit and .watch.

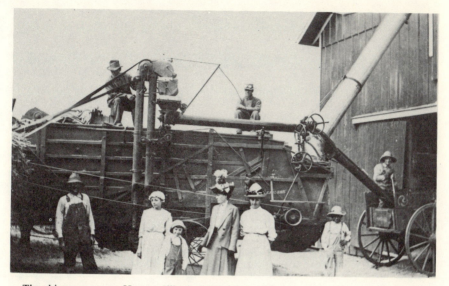

Threshing scene near Homer, Illinois (1911). Relatives from town, come to watch the harvesting, have brought a snapshot camera.

Sometimes town people lived in the country. Of course, only those who could afford the carriage and equipage necessary to commute did so. A large country estate, landscaped as a park but otherwise run as a farm, could be found immediately outside many towns. There lived the town banker, or the family whose predecessors had originally promoted the town and whose investments still dominated many of the town's businesses.

Country roads beckoned the town boy to fish, to hunt, or simply to tramp the woods looking for excitement. The country road with barefoot boys, dogs, and fishing poles was an important part of early twentieth century small-town iconography. Theodore Drieser writes of ''the stillness of the woods, the novelty of a long bamboo pole and a white line and red and green cork, a hook, worms, [and] the nibble of the unseen creature below the yellow surface of the stream,'' based on his childhood experiences. He continues: ''I see a dragon fly, steely blue and gauze of wing, fluttering and shimmering above my cork. . . . And then late in the afternoon, after hours of this wonderful world, we trudge home, along the warm, dusty, yellow country road; the evening sun is red in the west. . . . Brown-legged, dusty, tired, we tramp back to the kitchen door.''[42]

Rural roads were a favorite subject for small-town photographers in

Farmhouse near Perrysville, Indiana (circa 1910). Wealthy farmers frequently invested in businesses in nearby towns, as the more affluent bankers and merchants often invested in nearby farms. Large houses at the edge of town symbolized this conjunction of rural and urban interests. The family was comfortable in its pastoral setting, yet the conveniences of town life were also immediately accessible.

Rural road near Covington, Indiana (1912). The postcards which sold in drugstores and other places stereotyped towns and their localities. Nothing represented the town's connection to its surrounding countryside like two boys going fishing along a country pike. The message on the back of the card reads: "Here we are safe and sound headed for the East. We are now resting on the square viewing the sights. We passed through a covered bridge over the Wabash River. Having a grand time."

quest of marketable images for postcards. Often photographers doctored scenes to make roads look even more idyllic, more pastoral than they really were. The telephone poles might be masked with only their cross bars remaining like ghosts in the treetops, as in the 1912 photograph from Wisconsin.

Pictures where roads crossed rivers or skirted lakes, or where the trees arched nearly obscuring the sky, were the most romantic. Page Smith notes that in every recollection of the town one finds water used as a symbol:

> In its classic form it is the old swimming hole or the broad Mississippi of Tom Sawyer or Huck Finn. It is the symbol of freedom and also for mystery and perhaps for something deeper. In the swimming hole, clothes and the conventions of the town are discarded. The adult world is rejected in this unique arena which custom has allowed as the American boy's special preserve. The pond, the lake, the river, the swamp, the stream; it is as though here the small town boy is dimly aware that he touches the source of life—dangerous, strangely loving and enfolding.[43]

Even grown men could be boys at the river or the lake.

Rural road near Delevan, Wisconsin (1912). Photographers often doctored pictures to increase their value as stereotyped images. In this photograph the telephone poles have been partially obscured to increase the scene's pastoral quality.

Rural roads beckoned the townspeople out of town, but only for short distances and only during the summer months since the roads were poor, and the range of the horse-drawn carriage was limited. While the electric interurban railroads flourished, people in many towns could ride the cars to nearby cities or to picnic sites in parks developed by the traction companies. Near Homer, Illinois, a covered bridge, a prime symbol of pastoral environment, was preserved in the local traction park. Pastoralism could be and was packaged for leisure time. Boating was popular: it was an easy way to preserve dress and decorum, yet experience river and lake environments in a novel way.

Fishing near Homer, Illinois (circa 1910). Water was an important small-town icon. Creeks, rivers, and lakes were places of escape—places of renewal within easy reach of the town.

Camping was less popular than picnicking but, nonetheless, an activity engaged in by at least a few in every town. Churches established campgrounds to promote socializing and conduct Christian education in settings divorced from normal routines. Church camps often developed into elaborate grounds serving not just local congregations but whole regions, as at Winona Lake, Indiana. A town's economy could be substantially affected by a summer population attracted to these camps and lodges. City people used the camps as means of regaining idealized rural environments.

The Chautauqua was another summer institution which thrived in American small towns in the early twentieth century. It was organized in New York State, but spread throughout the country. Each participating town organized a week-long celebration of lectures and musical programs calculated to uplift the community culturally. The Chautauqua won both praise and condemnation. Advocates saw it as a mechanism for enlightenment as its founder had intended: ''Self improvement in all our faculties,

Holiday excursion on the interurban railroad near Homer, Illinois (1912). The interurban cars took small towners to parks created by the traction companies.

Traction park near Homer, Illinois (circa 1915). The ideal park mixed the "wilder"
icons of water and woods with icons of pastoral seclusion such as covered bridges.

Boating near Galena, Illinois (circa 1910). Fishing was a sport for adults as swimming was for children, especially boys. But boating and canoeing were family entertainments. A boat adrift on a stream also provided privacy for couples.

Family camping, location unknown (circa 1910). The out-of-doors promised renewed health and vitality, especially for husbands who relaxed while wives pursued their ordinary household activities under primitive conditions.

Bible camp at Winona Lake, Indiana (circa 1915). Many Protestant denominations operated bible camps—an activity with roots in early nineteenth century camp meetings. Many resort towns, like Winona Lake, began by catering to church groups.

Bible camp at Winona Lake, Indiana (circa 1915). The larger camps were miniature towns, complete with parades down simulated "Main Streets."

for us all, through all time, for the greatest good of all people." He had seen a "divine idea, a democratic idea, a people's idea, a progressive idea, a millenial idea."[44] Critics saw the Chautauqua as hucksterism in which the client was misled: "He is sold the idea that by paying $1.80 for five days of Chautauqua, he can get himself a liberal education, a whole carload of canned culture. It is infinitely easier than trying to think."[45]

Chautauqua grounds at Shelbyville, Illinois (circa 1915). The cultural isolation felt in small towns distant from sophisticated metropolises encouraged the Chautauqua. Lectures, musical programs, and craft demonstrations promised a brief period of mental uplifting each summer.

Chautauqua week was something short of a festival. Theodore Dreiser found the streets of North Manchester, Indiana, hung with banners: "In the store windows were . . . pictures of Stomboli the celebrated band leader, a chrysanthemum haired, thin bodied Italian in a braided white suit, who had been photographed crouching, as though he were about to spring, and with one thin hand raised high in the air holding a baton."[46] Many towns, like Shelbyville in Illinois, built large pavilions in landscaped parks to house Chautauqua activities.

A few towns were resort towns. Most of these were oriented to some environmental amenity—mineral waters, lake or ocean beach, mountain scenery, warm winter weather. Most resorts were creatures of the railroads or, as in the case of Saugatuck, Michigan, of the steamship lines. Saugatuck featured a large dance pavilion, hotels, and guest houses. During the summer months the steamboats brought thousands of tourists from Chicago each evening. One hotel was a converted sawmill from the time when Saugatuck was a lumber town. Tourism was the savior of more than one declining mine or mill town with the good fortune to enjoy an

View of Saugatuck, Michigan (1915). Through the 1930s passenger ships arrived each evening from Chicago, joined occasionally by larger cruise ships. Saugatuck made its water orientation into a successful resort business. Resort towns gave the big-city resident a special taste of American small-town life, and served as stepping-stones to "wilder places" beyond.

A curiosity of Key West, Florida (1913). Vacationers from Indiana have contrived a picture to impress friends and relatives back home.

93

unusual setting attractive to visitors. Resorts prospered because they offered the public unique experiences, something out of the ordinary.

Conclusion

There was security in the recurrent patterns of small-town life. Daily, weekly, and seasonal cycles brought some variety, but these changes were ordered and easily predicted. Life did not change so rapidly as to be threatening to the established social order of things, nor to the individual's place in that order. The scale of the small town was easily understood. Life did not proceed under pressure, nor was it mystifyingly complex, as some people in the cities complained. Life appeared to be comfortable for most small towners.

Leisure time was emphasized in the photographs people sent each other. Next to pictures of Main Street and one another's houses, the most plentiful variety of small-town photography depicted people at play. A Main Street clearly symbolized an entire town, for it was a scene readily recognized as belonging to the town. And of course people took pride in their houses, for these symbolized a family's life-style and general status in a community. But pictures of people at play also contained status inferences. Scenes along a lake or a river, or in the woods, suggested that those people lived in an interesting environment, and could afford the leisure time to enjoy it.

Novelists used time as they used place—to create settings or situations for plot and character development. They wove unusual events on the warp of the commonplace. Social scientists, especially those who wrote community case studies, also focused on common cycles—daily, weekly, seasonal. Both the novel and the community study tended to define small-town society as highly regularized, and small-town people as conforming to routine patterns of behavior. Photography, on the other hand, suggested that small-town people lived unhurried lives punctuated by frequent leisure-time diversions.

Photographs of pastoral and wilder scenes were an integral part of small-town iconography. Small towners saw their communities as rooted in agrarian hinterlands (as indeed they were in farming areas). The small town was thought to be in the midst of natural scenery. Thus the general model of the railroad town is enlarged to embrace these aspects of recreation and rural orientation—the fairground with its Chautauqua pavilion, the cottage settlement by the river, and the rural byways which served the town both as market roads and as paths of temporary escape.

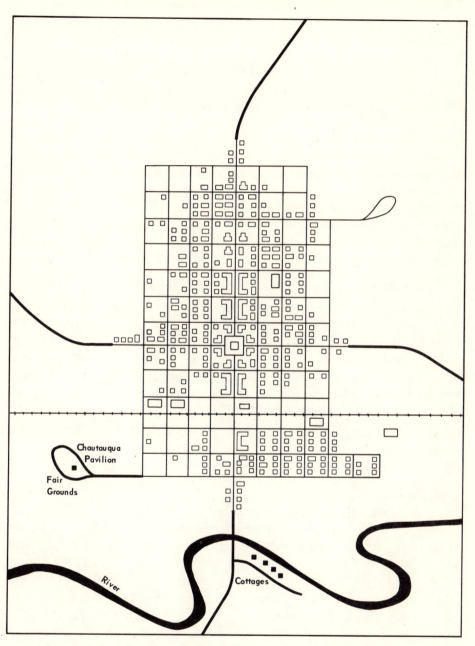

A hypothetical small town: recreational orientation before the automobile age.

Five

Small Towns and the Public Welfare

When Mrs. Etta Hewins, President of the W.C.T.U. here, swung an
ax on a seized whiskey still, the members of the society sang, "Praise
God, From Whom All Blessings Flow!"
Greencastle *Daily Banner*

A small town's social fabric was held together by formal social
organizations focused on specific activities, and often operated from
specific points of view. The various levels of government (town, county,
and federal), schools, churches, and various service clubs and fraternal
groups provided a social framework for neighboring, friendship, and kin-
ship. Together these organizations upheld the public welfare. Through
them conflict was resolved and consensus sometimes turned to action. As
these organizations had physical identity in the landscape, they did much
to symbolize a sense of community for small-town people.

Government

Town Government

Most towns ran their own affairs under municipal charters granted by
the state. In smaller places town government usually provided only essen-
tial services such as police and fire protection, street maintenance, and
street lighting. Independent boards ran the schools, and usually the library
and parks. In the larger places government often provided water and
sewage systems in addition. Town government varied, with a mayor and
town council here and a commissioner or even a town manager there. In
New England, town or township government combined municipal and
county functions.

According to Thorstein Veblen, most town governments were run by
business interests variously oriented to land speculation: "The location of
any given town has commonly been determined by collusion between
'interested parties' with a view to speculation in real estate, and [the town]
continues through its life-history . . . to be managed as a real estate 'prop-

osition.'" In paving Main Street a local government acted to enhance the value of business property; in increasing fire and police protection, insurance rates were lowered and businesses made more profitable. Veblen concludes: "Its municipal affairs, its civic pride, its community of interest, converge upon its real estate values, which are invariably of a speculative character, and which all its loyal citizens are intent on 'booming' and 'boosting.'"[1]

Sherwood Anderson describes a typical council meeting in *Hello Towns*. Mr. King of the National Bank urges settlement of his bill for constructing a sidewalk in front of his bank. Mr. Wheeler complains of the water leaking from the railroad's water tank. Committees are appointed to investigate new fire hydrants and the installation of a "great white way" on Main Street.[2] Town improvement was viewed largely in terms of an enhanced business environment. According to Newell Sims, the residents of "Aton," Indiana, took little interest in town government until improvements on Main Street began.[3] Citizens then sought to extend utilities and other services into the better residential areas, if not throughout the town. Business and professional men gave the typical town its leadership in such ventures.

Industry, frugality, equality, neighborliness, and loyalty were conspicuous components of the town's ideology in the nineteenth century. But new philosophies came to dominate in the twentieth century. The philosophy of "looking out for yourself," a calculating shrewdness, the ability to drive a hard bargain were emphasized, instead of cooperation and mutual helpfulness. Page Smith ties the change of small-town values to increased land speculation and "get rich quick" schemes of sharp business practice which "loosened personal morality and depersonalized individual relationships." Thus American "individualism" appeared only after the older community values had been eroded by big-city values. In this way, according to Smith, small-town leaders adopted the values of the city.[4]

Small-town leadership usually fell to city-bred or at least city-trained businessmen, doctors, lawyers, teachers, ministers, and others whose ambition was to make the small town "progressive."[5] Rarely did they fully succeed. Progressive tendencies were easily countered by basic small-town conservatism rooted in the ethic of good neighboring. Thorstein Veblen writes: "One must eschew opinions, or information, which are not acceptable to the common run. . . . The country-town system of knowledge and belief can admit nothing that would annoy the prejudices of any appreciable number of respectable townsfolk. So it becomes a system of intellectual, institutional, and religious holdovers. The country town is conservative, aggressively and truculently so."[6]

A town hall was usually located on a side street just off Main Street or the courthouse square. Real estate capable of generating tax money was thus reserved for business. The courthouse brought people to town, which was good for business; thus the courthouse was given an honored place. But the town hall was a fixture of no significance to trade and it could be shunted aside. In New England, on the other hand, the town hall functioned much like a courthouse. It usually occupied a highly visible location beside a village green or park. The town hall was often grouped with the buildings of other institutions like the grange or the Congregational Church, as in Williamsburg, Massachusetts.

Town center at Williamsburg, Massachusetts (circa 1900). Community was clearly symbolized in most New England towns where town halls and churches (and often grange and fraternal hall as well) faced a village green. The same pattern was also found in upstate New York and parts of the upper Midwest, where New Englanders had settled in the nineteenth century. The green with its community facilities was an obvious attraction to postcard makers.

The town hall in Farmer City, Illinois, contained a council chamber on the second floor and town offices on the first floor, including the police and fire station. Most fire departments were volunteer organizations—truly influential organizations in the politics of the town. Such volunteer groups served as social clubs as well as performing vital public service. Many towns clustered public facilities, with the water tower, fire station, and town hall standing together as in Pittsfield, Illinois. In the smaller towns without complete water systems, the tower supplied only the fire hydrants and the tower and fire station were functionally linked.

Novelists made occasional use of the small-town water tower. In William Faulkner's *The Town*, the tower symbolizes Flem Snope's rise from boiler tender to bank president.[7] Flem strips the power plant of its brass fittings and hides them in the water tower for later sale. This step in his rise to power was devious, but it was also open for all to see if only

Town hall at Farmer City, Illinois (circa 1915). The municipal auditorium next door was leased as a motion picture theater. Opera houses and fraternal halls located above Main Street stores were decreed unsafe for movies due to the fire hazard associated with early movie projectors.

Water standpipe at Pittsfield, Illinois (circa 1910). Skylines in more progressive towns were dominated by water towers. Church spires competed for ascendancy in New England, and grain elevators in the Midwest.

99

town residents had been more alert to the tower above them. Homer Croy writes in *West of the Water Tower*: "The tower was a town character; the city revolved around it almost as much as around the court house, or around the square. Picnic parties were held at its base; boys climbed up the little iron ladder, which seemed to reach to infinity, as high as courage lasted and scratched a chalk mark on the red brick; then the next boy tried to raise it."[8] Larry Woiwode remembers the water tower in his hometown of Hyatt, North Dakota, for his brother "once climbed it and peed from the top."[9] Perhaps the water tower, like town government itself, was too self-evident to receive close attention.

A town usually took pride in its park, even when that park filled space originally intended for a courthouse. At Oakes, North Dakota, the town fathers planted trees, shrubs, and flower beds; sprinklers kept the grass green. A gigantic flagpole was located at the center of the open square with the bandstand nearby. A reflecting pool, drinking fountain, and benches completed the park's furnishings. At Farmer City, Illinois, the park also occupied a square with Main Street business extending to the south. Here were symbols of both past and future: the Civil War cannon sat to one side; a lamp of the "great white way" stood in the center of the walk. Additional light standards lined both sides of Main Street. Town parks were resting places where idlers sat to survey people entering and leaving Main Street. They were convenient places for reunions, rallies, and

Town park at Oakes, North Dakota (1924). The park provided a buffer between downtown businesses and the more affluent residential area of Oakes. The automobile has made its appearance: a gasoline station stands at the corner, and down the street beyond the curbside pump a sign advertises the Oakes Auto and Machine Co., an early automobile dealer. Automobiles stand at the curb where horses once flourished.

all the other celebrations for which people gathered. Like courthouse squares, parks served as ritual places to enhance the sense of local community.

Park at Farmer City, Illinois (circa 1915). This park was tied into Main Street by the new light standards of the "great white way"—clusters of five globes used to illuminate both streets and business facades. "Great white ways" symbolized progress.

County Government

The courthouse was usually a county seat's most elaborate landmark as it symbolized both town and country, certain functions of county government extending to both. The county (or parish in Louisiana) maintained rural roads and provided police protection beyond the town. But a county's most important function was to house the local court. Before the automobile so altered commuting patterns, rural people flocked to town when court was in session. An especially notorious trial found the courthouse yard thronged with people. Many farm families, come to share in the general excitement, camped by their wagons.

Many counties lavished money on expensive court buildings, which were intended to symbolize county government and not just provide space for county functions. Second Empire and Romanesque Revival styles in architecture gave way to neoclassical and Depression Modern designs after 1900. Courthouse renovations sometimes produced a mixture of styles in a single building as at Oskaloosa, Iowa.

County offices were arranged on the first floor of the typical court building. Here people bought marriage licenses, paid taxes, and searched for deeds and birth certificates. Courtrooms and judges' chambers were on the upper floors. When court was not in session, courthouses were often quite deserted. Theodore Dreiser walked through one in southern Indiana "only to see the county treasurer, or someone in his office, sawing away on a fiddle."[10] Perhaps no single individual personified county government more than the sheriff, the town's principal figure of law and order. The jail was either in the courthouse or in a separate building nearby.

Courthouse at Oskaloosa, Iowa (1938). The older Romanesque Revival styling of the building's base contrasts with the modern renovation of its tower. After World War I the small towner's quest to be up-to-date, reinforced by designers and material suppliers, brought change to many small-town structures both public and private.

Federal Government

In the larger towns the post office was an elaborate building nearly equalling the courthouse in style, but rarely in size. Neoclassical designs showing the influence of the European-derived "Beaux Arts" typified the larger towns after World War I. In the smaller towns the post office often occupied a storefront or one part of a store. Most post offices were built privately to specified guidelines, and leased by the federal government over a long term. Thus the Postal Service stood to influence small-town tastes in architecture through its design dictates.

Widespread use of neoclassical designs for small-town post offices paralleled their popularity in Washington, D.C. They symbolized the increased involvement of the federal government in small-town and rural affairs. The county extension agent (tied to a state land-grant university) was subsidized by the federal government. Many counties had offices of the Soil Conservation Service after Franklin Roosevelt's New Deal. Federal offices were often housed in the basement of the post office, dubbed the federal building in many places.

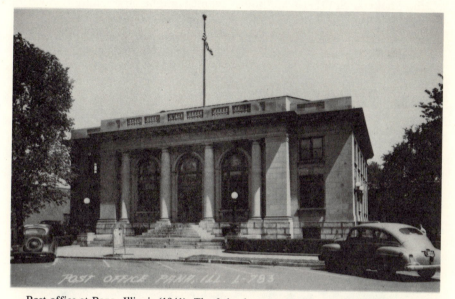

Post office at Pana, Illinois (1941). The federal government was symbolized more substantially in small towns after World War I, with the construction of elaborate post offices in larger places. The American flag widely displayed throughout a town was a constant reminder of nationhood.

Churches

Churches not only served a town's spiritual needs, but they were also important places for socializing. In "Aton," Newell Sims found that the churches exerted community-wide influence: "The church was easily the most dominant social force . . . leading reforms, promoting improvements, and directing pleasure."[11] Church influence was exerted through its members as they molded opinion and made decisions in other settings. A community's churches set a moral tone. In "Aton" the pool halls and saloons were not patronized by "religious men" for "such things set an example 'that hurts the church.'"[12] Church membership varied from town to town and over time within any given community, but almost everywhere it was heavily weighted in favor of older residents, especially women.[13]

Small-town churches were quite status conscious at the turn of the century. Charles Givens writes of the fictional Tennessee town of "Tirus":

The Southern Methodist women were as far above Northern
Methodist women as Queen Mary was above the corner greengrocer's
wife. Southern Methodists were professional people and the well-to-
do farmers. Then came the Baptists and Presbyterians, the Northern
Methodists, and finally far down the line, the Holiness Church and
the Shakers. Southern Methodist women might be friendly enough
with Baptists and Presbyterians, and Northern Methodists. But there
was a certain distinction, always felt and shown. And no Southern
Methodist woman ever spoke to a Holiness Churcher except as to a
servant.[14]

Cornerstone laying at a new church, town unknown (circa 1900). Although the few
males in the photograph actually set the stone, females and children of both sexes
dominated the crowd, as they did church attendance in most small towns.

In the North, a town's Episcopalians, Presbyterians, Methodists, Baptists,
and Catholics usually ranked in that order along the social status scale.

Sunday services brought a flood of people to churches at the downtown edge. Booth Tarkington describes the procession in the fictional
town of "Canaan":

The intermittent procession stretched along the new cement sidewalks
from a little below the Square to Main Street, where maples lined the
thoroughfare and the mansions of the affluent stood among pleasant
lawn and shrubbery. The men imparted largely a gloom to the itin-
erant concourse, most of them wearing hot, long black coats and having wilted their collars; the ladies relieving this gloom somewhat by the
lighter tints of their garments; the spic-and-span little girls relieving it
greatly by their white dresses and their faces, the latter bright with the
hope of Sunday ice-cream.[15]

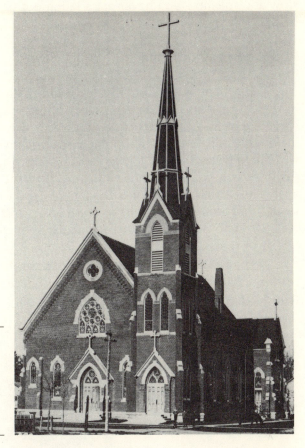

Church, town unknown (circa 1910). Churches competed with one another for members. The symbolism of church architecture played an important role. Taken together, a town's church towers symbolized a special morality within the larger community.

    Congregations competed with one another for members, and thus for influence in a community. Old buildings were modernized to keep pace with those of other congregations. New buildings symbolized the truly successful church: laying the cornerstone for a new building was an event of considerable importance. In the North the Roman Catholics often built the largest churches, complete with tall belfry towers topped with large crosses. In many parts of the Northeast and Midwest the majority of a town's artisans and laborers were Catholic. Their labor and their money poured into church designs commissioned through central church authorities. This was another important external force shaping both small-town architecture and small-town tastes in architecture. Protestants were quick to meet the Roman Catholic competition with elaborate churches of their own. On Sunday mornings congregations also competed with their church bells. R. L. Duffus recalls an early job as bell ringer in Waterbury, Vermont. He was instructed in the art by the church sexton: " 'You listen to the way church bells are rung around this town,' he pursued, 'and you'll get the idea. The Methodists are no good at all—too tinny, and they don't give a damn how it sounds to anybody but Methodists. Catholics are too slow and solemn—you never get a laugh out of a Roman Catholic church bell.' ''[16]

In Sickness and in Death

The general practitioner was a small-town institution. Smaller towns have never had sufficient population to justify specialization across a wide spectrum of medical practice. Only larger towns have been able to support hospital facilities, the smaller places making do with small clinics or going without. The doctor was a neighbor. He was a highly respected member of the town community for his education, and for his ability to comfort and heal. The carriage of the ''family doctor'' was a common sight on a town's streets and along rural roads as the doctor called upon the sick. The doctor's office upstairs over the drugstore or in some other location was a haven to the ill.

Death came frequently to the small-town family in the early twentieth century. Death rates were high without modern medicines and with less attention than now paid to sanitation and public health generally. Infant

A photograph of an infant (1921). The body was brought to a photographer's studio before burial. Death affected the small town through the network of intensive neighboring.

mortality ran between 10 and 15 percent during the twentieth century's first decade. The life expectancy of a male born in 1900 was 46.3 years, and of a female 48.3 years.[17] Nearly every small-town family of the period lost at least one child to disease. The rituals of death were elaborate. As small-town people neighbored intensively, a death in the community excited widespread sympathy and grief. Cemeteries, as the final resting place for the dead, were carefully contrived.

Cemetery at Portville, New York (1913). Photographers rarely ventured to the town cemetery, except to record special events such as the dedication of a public monument.

Cemeteries were really intended for the living as memorials to relatives and friends departed. They were parklike—often laid out to symbolize a utopian, pastoral ideal. Romantic and picturesque, they were often the best planned and most visually attractive part of town. Roads curved through a landscape of grass, trees, and shrubbery punctuated by grave markers. Here the "best" families continued their competition of ostentation by building private mausoleums or otherwise decorating family plots with elaborate statuary. Duffus writes of Waterbury, Vermont: "Our cemetery extended over a ridge back of the Congregational Church, running over toward the river. The older families had plots large enough to serve them for several generations in that slowly growing community. Newer families had to bury their dead along the edges, where the land began to slope down toward Winooski Street."[18]

Most cemeteries had a decorative centerpiece—an elaborate gate, gatehouse, or small chapel. The Civil War monument was in the cemetery, if not on the courthouse lawn or in a downtown park. A monument's dedication—as in Portville, New York, in 1913—brought a large crowd, prime among them the town's war veterans. In New England the Civil War was called "The Great Rebellion," and in the South "The War Between the States." By whatever name it was known, most towns, North and South, remembered the conflict with public architecture. The Civil War monument was usually the only piece of public sculpture in a community. After World War I most towns maintained an "honor roll," upon which the names of those who had fought in the nation's various wars were inscribed. Veterans' organizations usually took charge of maintaining the display—whether it be the painted wall of a business building, a glass-enclosed case on the courthouse lawn, or a bronze plaque at the cemetery.

The Library

The town library symbolized culture. It might be tax supported, but it was more than just a branch of town or county government. The library was nurtured by the community. A special group, called "The Friends of the Library" or something similar, looked after its affairs. The library functioned in part with volunteer labor; its books and buildings were often a gift to the community. Sometimes a prominent family donated the facili-

Public library at Neenah, Wisconsin (circa 1940). The library was an icon of community symbolizing cultural ambition beyond the ordinary. It linked the town with the world of ideas.

ty, but as often as not the money was given by residents from all classes. A library was something that nearly everyone agreed benefited the community. However, its impact could not be measured in dollars and cents and adequate support was not always forthcoming from local government.

The philanthropy of Andrew Carnegie enabled many communities to improve and enlarge their libraries. Between 1898 and 1917 Carnegie donated forty million dollars for library construction in 1,412 American communities.[19] Most of the money went to small towns, as the vast majority of the buildings were constructed for under twenty thousand dollars apiece. Most small-town libraries sported neoclassical design and followed closely the standardized Carnegie plan even when Carnegie money was not

Public library at Rugby, Tennessee (circa 1930).

used. One entered the typical building through a ceremonial portico of Grecian pillars. The large reading room was divided between adult's and children's sections. A public lecture hall was in the basement.

The town library was a storehouse of knowledge, a ready place of reference. It was also a place of entertainment, for reading was a primary source of relaxation before the age of radio and television. The library was female dominated. The librarian was usually a dedicated but underpaid woman. Most patrons were married women, although their visits might serve the reading habits of husbands and children as well. The library was perhaps the only place in town where one could venture regularly in search of both change of scene and intellectual stimulation. It was an interface with the outside world of ideas.

Schools

Schools not only served to educate a town's children, but played broad social and economic roles as well. They were a focus of community life and ritual. The business of education made a significant economic impact, especially in smaller places. The schools might employ dozens of teachers and thus control the biggest payroll in town. School buildings usually represented a capital investment in the millions of dollars.[20] For towns without a courthouse, the public school was usually the largest building. Throughout the South, and in many northern communities as well, a separate school served the black community. Black schools were usually inferior, and visibly so. They clearly symbolized the disadvantages of being "colored."

Towns supported their schools, but often grudgingly. Schools did not pay immediate financial returns and could not be championed like successful businesses. Attempts made to broaden curricula or introduce new teaching strategies were often suspect. School personnel usually came from outside the town and were questionable on that ground alone. Most small towners sought only limited objectives in supporting their schools. James West writes of "Plainville" as late as the 1940s:

> The most common adult phrasings in Plainville of the aims of formal schooling are (1) "to learn children readin', writin', and 'rithmetic and maybe a little joggerfy"; (2) "to give our children the same kind of education and the same chance that children have anywhere"; (3) "to keep children out of the way and out of trouble until they get old enough to know how to act"; and (4) "to keep children from growing up as wild and ignorant as animals."[21]

Public school at Homer, Illinois (circa 1910). Not all commercial postcards were made by local photographers; traveling photographers from city studios provided much of the postcard art. The back of this card is labeled: "Genuine Photo by C. U. Williams, Bloomington, Ill." City studios helped stereotype small towns.

The class photograph has been an American institution for several generations. Annually children lined up with their peers to have a likeness recorded for posterity. These photographs were shared with relatives and became permanent fixtures in family albums. Class photographs made good public relations for the school. For poorer families the school photographs often represented the only visual record of young children growing up. The hometown school remained a part of every child even in adulthood, as it was an integral part of growing up.

Public school at Brazil, Indiana (1910). When late in life adults remembered the names of their grade-school classmates, they demonstrated the extent to which their hometowns could be imprinted on youthful minds.

Schools changed. Early buildings were usually little more than large frame or brick boxes. Rose Wilder Lane writes:

> Two storied with unshaded windows regularly spaced on all sides, it rose gaunt above an irregular space of trodden earth on which not a spear of grass survived. Its height was increased and seemed unbalanced by the cupola rising from the eaves above the door. A large bell hung there, and when The Principal pulled the rope in the entry below, that bell clanged an iron imperative over the town. It was the voice of a place austerely devoted to toil, permitting no frivolity and righteously crushing any impulse toward merriment or play.[22]

The growth of a town necessitated larger buildings. New regulations imposed by state governments forced expansion and continued modernization. The consolidation of rural and town school districts, accelerated

Public school at Ridge Farm, Illinois (circa 1920). Newness in the landscape symbolized vitality and progress worthy of the attention of the amateur as well as the professional photographer.

Girls' basketball team, town unknown (1908). Public schools symbolized local communities in many ways. Local pride was tied to the successes and failures of school athletic teams.

later by automobile travel on improved roads, prompted construction of larger buildings. Some new schools were in more accessible locations at the edge of town, but many new buildings rose in the rubble of the old. Towns sometimes had parochial schools in addition to the public variety: Roman Catholic schools were found where French Canadians, Poles, or Italians had settled in large numbers in New England; where Mexican-Americans lived in the Southwest; and where Germans were concentrated in the Midwest.

State Normal School at Gorham, Maine (circa 1920). The college town held a prominent place in the American scheme of higher education. Towns were thought by many to be ideal incubators for the nation's youth.

The public school contributed much to a town's identity. Organized sports at the high-school level—especially baseball, basketball, and football—pitted small-town teams against one another in an exercise of pride.

Some towns were college towns. A small college was like a mill or a factory in that it provided a service or a product to outsiders. It brought money into the locality. A local college served its town in other ways, too. Its faculty enlarged the educated sector of the population and provided additional leadership for the churches, social clubs, and local government. Local youths found college educations more accessible. A successful college often dominated the personality of a town, especially when the name of the college and the name of the town were one and the same—names like Amherst, Oberlin, Auburn, or Claremont. The idealized college campus was set on a hill at the edge of town, its buildings arranged in a parklike setting as at Gorham in Maine.

If the small town was an incubator of America's business and professional elites, as many claimed, then how appropriate that colleges, the incubators of future elites, be located in small-town environments. Most small-town colleges had been founded in the nineteenth century by Protestant denominations for training ministers and teachers. By 1900 most had been secularized, with the sciences their new and primary orientation. Page Smith notes that small, denominational, liberal-arts colleges educated far more prominent scientists in proportion to their total graduates than larger state universities in the early twentieth century.[23] After examining the origins of American scientists, two commentators conclude: "Protestant orthodoxy and the psychology of the small town engendered an ideal of professional 'calling,' a fluidity of social organization, and an ethic of service to the larger good that, in an increasingly materialistic and secular society, made science a most attractive field for young men." In addition, they see small-town environments as encouraging attributes of character, among them strong individualistic incentives to achievement, pragmatism, democratic ideology, rationalism, and empiricism of outlook as well as sobriety, thrift, and other fundamental Protestant virtues.[24]

Business district at Burke, Idaho, on Friday the 13th. Few townscapes escaped the ravages of fire, although the loss of an entire business district was rare after the post-World War I adoption of motorized fire-fighting equipment in most towns.

Coping with Disaster

Small-town institutions were geared to the ordinary routines of life. But to nearly every town there came disasters, big and small, striking without warning. Disasters not only affected landscapes and human lives, but the subsequent efforts to return to normal altered community institutions. Should a college building be destroyed, the college might be

114

threatened with closing. Jobs would be lost and the community's income reduced. Such emergencies were usually faced informally. Friendships across a spectrum of relevant government and private institutions were used to solve problems in an ad hoc fashion. A fund-raising drive, donated labor and equipment, or the loan of facilities might be arranged. The climate of small-town neighboring greatly simplified such activity. Immediate reaction to disaster also followed the impulse of personalized neighboring—neighbors helping neighbors with relatives close at hand.

Public school blaze, town unknown (circa 1910).

Fire was a recurring problem. Few Main Streets escaped a major blaze longer than a decade. Many towns lost entire business districts to fire as at Burke, Idaho. The back of the postcard of this disaster reads: "This was the business district. People didn't even have time to get a few clothes. It went so fast they had all they could do to get out alive." Massive destruction by fire was the price many towns paid for the pedestrian convenience of densely built business districts. Other intensively used places, especially public buildings, were also vulnerable to fire. The primitive fire-fighting equipment and the volunteer fire departments of the early twentieth century were no match for large blazes.

Fire raced quickly through frame buildings with their varnished floors and wooden interiors, as shown in the accompanying photograph. The fire has spread rapidly; the children and their teachers have fled into the winter cold leaving their coats behind. They have stood to watch the building consumed with fire and now they run for the warmth of nearby buildings. The fire department has not yet arrived. Such disasters produced a town's most dramatic moments. To be awakened on a winter's

115

night by the clanging of the fire bell, and to see outside an orange pall cast upon the landscape by a nearby blaze—such moments set the heart pounding with the mixed sensations of fear and excitement.

Harold Sinclair's novel, *Years of Illusion,* begins with a late night fire in the business district of a large town. As the destruction spread from building to building, people assembled downtown to watch. The firefighters were hopelessly overwhelmed. Men retreated to the taverns for a last drink: "They Goddamned and by-Godded and fished in their pockets for more silver to buy more drinks or stood morose and silent over their glasses while behind them the holocaust roared on."[25] Other men with businesses and offices downtown sought to salvage their valuables. John Ranson, the book's principal character, rescued files from his law office located across from the courthouse: "When he had hoisted the bundle to a shoulder he paused for a moment, taking what might be a last look around the dingy office which had served both his father and grandfather. They had sat in these chairs, written their names innumerable times at these tables and desks, planned this and that in these rooms." The entire business district was consumed. "Valuable and only partially insured stocks of merchandise, some of it still unpaid for, had vanished into the air; law libraries, sometimes the gatherings of years, were gone in smoke; the instruments and office equipment of physician after physician had disappeared, become twisted or melted lying with heaps of debris in basements."[26]

Disasters were important landmarks in time for small-town people. A town's calamities shone like beacons in the haze of recollection which passed as town history. More importantly, the big fire or flood or tornado often proved an important turning point in a town's development. The community that could not muster capital for reinvestment or other forms of cooperation toward rebuilding lost its vitality. But the town that pooled resources as a community usually came back stronger than before. When a town's institutions cooperated toward common goals, then collective welfare was well served.

Conclusion

The courthouse, town hall, post office, park, church, cemetery, library, and school not only symbolized vital community functions, but the community itself. The general model of the hypothetical small town is modified once again to reflect this fact. Most small towners took pride in their community's public environment. The scale and character of public buildings greatly influenced what one saw and remembered in a given place. The size of a park or the upkeep given the school grounds suggested much about the people who lived in a town. Local government and the

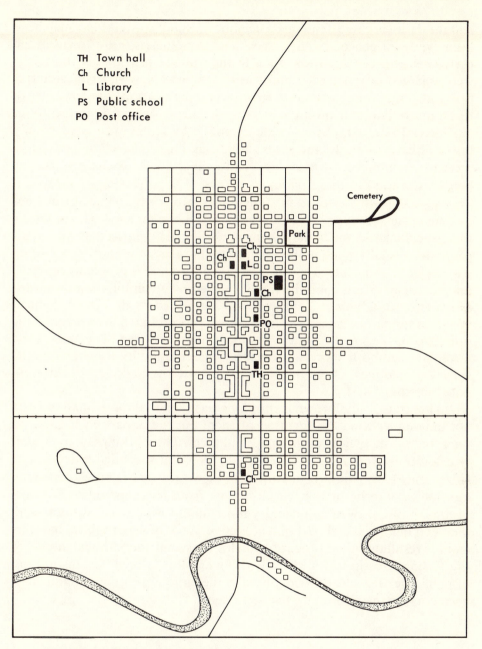

A hypothetical small town: public sector before the automobile age.

churches had much to do with the appearance of things. Propriety was a small-town trait, and much energy was expended to insure that the public environment looked modern, efficient, and interesting.

Perhaps business interests did influence local government unduly. Maybe towns were inherently conservative, due to intensive neighboring

117

and the desire not to offend one's neighbors. Small-town leaders may have been overly influenced by big-city values. Nonetheless, most towns in the early twentieth century took pride in their public institutions. Buildings were enlarged or replaced to meet new demands. New styles of architecture and design were introduced to reflect modernization. The town strove to be up-to-date and progressive. Appeareances figured prominently in commercial photography as pride in public buildings translated readily into postcard sales. Pictures of public buildings, churches, and parks served to symbolize towns as distinctive places, and to characterize the people who lived in those places.

A small town's institutions functioned informally. All problems, not just emergencies, tended to be solved in an ad hoc manner. The influence of key personalities made the system work. Social organizations were comprised of partially overlapping memberships, the same individuals often playing leadership roles across a spectrum of groups. A problem confronting one organization could be rapidly solved by a combination of groups as requests for advice and aid were communicated by the relatively small set of community leaders. A cohesive and coordinated view toward the problems of the small-town environment often emerged. The small-town novel lavished both success at business and community leadership on its heros and heroines. Often the two kinds of success could not be differentiated in story lines.

The scale of small-town institutions was such that most small towners not only understood the function of each, but the impact each made on them and the daily lives of those around them. The workings of community institutions were not mysterious; they were not shrouded in secrecy. A citizen may have paid little attention to the workings of church and state, but not because he or she felt closed off from local institutions. At the beginning of the twentieth century most small towners felt at home with their communities, and part of a collective. Lack of geographical mobility and the resultant inward focus of small towns contributed substantially to this feeling. Gossip travelled easily, keeping all informed. The institutions of public welfare, clearly symbolized in the buildings of church and state, served as magnets for collective sentiment.

Six

The Automobile and Its Initial Impact

> The tempo picked up and he noticed men didn't like to wait any more, they'd open up the [barbershop] door and hold on to it when they saw he was busy and somebody ahead of them, and say, "How long, Ben?" and he'd say how long and they'd say, "I'll be back," and wouldn't wait, or if they did it was in a fidgety way, and there was always an automobile waiting impatiently outside to rush them some other place, and they were in no mood to sing and their voices had lost the feel for good close harmony."
>
> Ferdinand Reyher, *I Heard Them Sing*

The automobile changed the small town. The tempo of life picked up as travel quickened and distances shrank. A family's prize possession was often its automobile, and work and recreation were altered in accommodation. The look of small towns changed. Streets were widened and otherwise improved. New enterprises oriented to the automobile joined older establishments along Main Street in the more successful towns. Elsewhere the automobile brought stagnation: as rural and small-town populations became increasingly mobile, people from the smaller towns drove to shop at larger places. The automobile made people less dependent upon the locality which had previously defined their community.

The New Automobile

The first automobile to reach a town always caused great excitement. Bruce Catton remembers the baseball game interrupted by the arrival of a motorcar: "The automobile stopped to see the game, and the game stopped to see the automobile."[1] Originally, the automobile was viewed as a luxury for a town's gentry. In 1910 twenty-five men in "Aton" owned automobiles, according to Newell Sims. "It's alright for those who can afford them, but some folks had better pay their debts and own a home before an automobile," was a comment frequently heard in "Aton" at the time.[2]

The desire to own an automobile was widespread, but so was the suspicion that to do so was somehow damaging. In "Plainville" the first cars were seen as ostentatious, impractical, extravagant, immoral to own, and dangerous. In addition, farmers viewed them as a threat to the value of horses and the market for grain sold as horse feed.[3] By the 1930s the benefits of increased geographical mobility and the prestige of car ownership had encouraged most families in most towns to buy automobiles. Art Gallaher comments on "Plainville" in the 1950s: "People are proud of a good car and there is prestige in owning a current model, particularly one of the more expensive makes."[4] But the person who bought "just for show" was still criticized. "His car don't impress me none," was still a frequent remark. It was common for young people to leave "Plainville" for city work to "bust themselves buyin' a new car" to bring home and "show off."[5]

Automobile ownership became a great new expense. It compelled lower-income people, especially an area's marginal farmers, to think more in terms of "money" rather than "subsistence."[6] Traditionally, farmers had battered farm products for merchandise: "On Saturdays they came to town, dressed for the occasion . . . bringing the week's surplus of butter, eggs, vegetables, and fruits. They came to the stores to trade."[7] The word *trade* lingered, although its meaning changed: people who never bartered eggs for calico would say, "I trade at so-and-so's," or "he gets my trade." Early in the century most "Plainvillers" operated in two separate and simultaneous economic systems, a "money economy" and a "subsistence economy." For example, the town doctor kept a large garden and raised hogs and a cow. For a quart of milk daily, a high-school boy fed and milked the doctor's cow as well as doing other chores.[8]

But bartered eggs and butter did not buy automobiles, nor for that matter the myriad other products widely advertised and universally desired such as appliances and radios. New cars cost hard, cold cash. People were forced away from subsistence and into the money economy. Farmers augmented their incomes with work in town and wives went to work to earn a second income. W. L. White remembers that "the fellow who kept the drug-store had a barber's chair in the back, and would leave anyone he was shaving for just a minute if another customer came in for medicine."[9] The exchange of services declined in the typical town, as did the sense of community it engendered. Increasingly time came to be viewed as money. James West observes: "Mutual helpfulness was greater when it cost only work, rather than money."[10]

The money economy loosened the ties of community in many ways. The automobile took people to jobs, shopping, and recreation in other places. Ferdinand Reyher writes that the automobile "seemed designed to loosen ties and dangle the horizon before the unsettled." More strangers were seen on the street, until they seemed to outnumber the people who were known. The pace of life was quickened. The decline of Ben Halper's barber shop in Reyher's "Sevillinois" was symptomatic.[11]

> It was coming to him hard and inescapable, the realization that the older barber shop was done for. The shrine of leisure and tolerance was no more. An automobile horn honked angrily at the corner, and others blared in irritable response. The automobile. It bred impatience. A man always had it on his mind. Standing outside, seemingly inert at the curb, but straining to go. The automobile was untouchable God.[12]

An automobile at Homer, Illinois (1918). Many writers of the period thought the automobile a boon to family connectedness. The Sunday drive out from town was an opportunity to be together, and entertainment for the entire family. In the long run, however, the automobile probably had the opposite influence by taking people away from home separately.

The importance of a family's car was clearly reflected in photograph albums. Suddenly it was popular to be photographed sitting in an automobile. The car enhanced a family's status, even when it precipitated its decline by taking its members more and more away from home. Automobile ownership soared. Registered motor vehicles in the United States climbed from 468,500 in 1910 to 9,230,000 in 1920.[13]

Changing Business Patterns

Improved automobiles and motor trucks, improved highways, and increased mechanization in farming brought profound changes to small-town retail and wholesale trades.[14] Farmers could drive to town and back in minutes, where hours had been required previously. They could spend more time in the larger places where the range of goods and services was greater, and where the larger volume of business reduced prices. Mechanization brought farm consolidation and the abandonment of marginal operations. As people left the land, markets declined and businessmen in the smaller towns found it increasingly difficult to stay in business. Economist A. H. Anderson calculates that in a half hour the typical farmer could travel about three miles in 1915, and fifteen miles in 1960.[15] A three-mile radius around a given town comprised thirty-six square miles, and a fifteen-mile radius comprised nine hundred square miles. Assuming a farm population of nine persons per square mile in 1915, and five persons in 1960, then each area would contain three hundred and thirty-three hundred persons, respectively. The larger, more viable towns stood to benefit from increased markets at the expense of smaller places.

By the 1930s the smaller towns across the country showed clear signs of business decline. Buildings were boarded up and abandoned along Main Street. But the Depression only hastened the inevitable. According to H. L. Mencken: "Where once a healthy activity could be noted one now observes a dull lethargy. There are few people on the streets, the store fronts look discouraged and uninviting . . . upon the faces of merchants and business men has settled a dull apathy to replace the once bright eagerness. . . . The old confidence, the old expectancy have vanished."[16] W. L. White writes of "Athena": "The business men were scared and hopeless. Hopeless, standing in empty stores looking out into the streets. Hopeless in unpressed suits and rattling five year-old cars. Hopeless with sunk mouths and tired, scared eyes."[17]

Of the thirty-two businesses in James West's "Plainville" of the mid-1940s, only six were considered "really paying propositions" by the townspeople: the undertaker, doctor, produce agent, Ford dealer, a grocer, and the owner of a liquor store prospered.[18] By 1960 a seventh profitable business had been added—a service station. "Plainville" was no longer a "night town" where formerly "there was always something going on" during the summer months.[19] Farmers no longer stayed into the evening nor did they tend to return after chores. Wives ran to town for daily needs, instead of buying on one big trading day. Above all, townspeople and farmers alike shopped more and more in larger, nearby towns and went more frequently to the nearby metropolis.

Although most large towns managed to hold their own with enlarged rural markets, they did not grow as rapidly as America's cities. *The American Mercury* reminded readers in 1934: "Towns below 10,000 population account for fifty-two percent of the entire population of the United States. They also account for forty-five percent of the entire number of retail establishments. Yet, with this population and this number of stores, they do but thirty percent of the total volume of retail business.[20]

The small-town merchant with a small inventory and slow turnover inevitably priced goods higher than did big-city competitors. In addition, the small-town tradition of extending credit made the cost of doing business approximately 10 percent higher. One's customers were also one's neighbors and had to be treated as such. Albert Blumenthal writes of "Mineville": "People demand to be treated as if they always meet all their obligations. And to refuse to give them credit is to drive them to [other stores]."[21] Intensive small-town neighboring rarely benefited the merchant. The businessmen who felt that locals should buy locally out of "loyalty to the town" were almost always disappointed. In "Plainville" residents saw their buying habits as a "dollar and cents matter," and loyalty to "Plainville" did not extend to their pocketbooks. Merchants complained: "All we can sell a lot of these people are minor items they forgot to buy in the city."[22]

Small-town retailing tried to follow big-city patterns. Stores necessarily stocked brand-name merchandise. Where once a grocer had simply offered flour as a generic item, now he carried specific brands advertised in the newspapers and on the radio. Gallaher writes that "Plainvillers" were constantly exposed to urban newspaper and radio advertising which promoted items generally available only in city stores.[23] But chain stores brought brand-name competition directly to the small-town merchant's front door. Chains expanded rapidly into America's small towns after 1910. For example, the Atlantic and Pacific Tea Company chain grew from 1,726 stores in 1915 to over 10,000 in 1923. Rockville, Indiana's "A & P" store precipitated a "bread war" in 1926 by cutting prices on bread below cost. This action not only diverted customers from more established stores, but closed the town's remaining roller mill. Bread arrived by truck at Rockville from cities up to seventy miles away.[24]

The urban orientation of small-town consumers was nothing new. The mail catalogue had always been a popular device for avoiding higher local prices and limited stocks. It was once a mark of defiance against the town merchant for a farmer to say, "I'll order it!"[25] By the 1920s catalogues lay on the counters of most stores for all to consult, with the merchant doing the ordering. But the automobile enabled customers to go frequently to the city, compare prices, and return with merchandise in hand.

Numerous devices were employed by small-town merchants to attract customers. Raffle tickets were distributed with purchases, and drawings held for free merchandise. Band concerts were sponsored in courthouse squares; movies were shown in vacant lots. Amateur baseball leagues were subsidized in hopes of attracting people to town on special market days when stores stayed open late. Special sales were held as shown in the photograph. The sign on the Fair Company Store reads: ''Big guinea race, Saturday June 21st, 10 a.m. $20 in merchandise given away. Absolutely free! Read details in circulars. Ask in store.''

A sales promotion, town unknown (circa 1925). Automobile travel greatly altered small-town trade areas, generally favoring larger over smaller centers. Merchants used lotteries, contests, and other devices to keep local customers ''at home.''

Many towns provided special facilities to encourage the farm trade. In Sinclair Lewis's *Main Street,* the women's club opened a rest room which helped symbolize for Carol Kennicott the sterility of the town:

> The rest-room resembled a second hand store. It was furnished with discarded patent rockers, lopsided reed chairs, a scratched pine table, a gritty straw mat, old steel engravings of milkmaids being morally amorous under willow-trees, faded chromos of roses and fish, and a kerosene stove for warming lunches. The front window was darkened by torn net curtains and by a mound of geraniums and rubber plants.[26]

Here farmer's wives could rest while their husbands ran errands or dawdled in the town's saloons.

Farm wives spent more time in town after the arrival of the automobile. The farm family began to feel more a part of the town, and through the town more a part of the new urban-oriented American dream. Concern with regional and national news, city tastes in clothing, and other manifestations of urban life spread through towns to farms as never before. One photograph shows a farm wife bringing home her groceries.

Her little girl grips a new coloring book and a "big city" newspaper.

Towns ignored the farmers only at their peril. "I am not interested in farmers," said the banker. "Our farmer business does not amount to anything." "Who is your largest depositor?" asked the newspaper man. "Why, the International Harvestor dealer," he answered.[27] But more often a town's business community knew where its bread was buttered. In Rosland, South Dakota, 50 percent of gross farm income was spent in town for fuel, tractors, machinery, buildings, labor, taxes, interest, and other expenses. Another 20 percent of gross was spent for feed and livestock purchases.[28] Joseph Lyford observed in Vandalia, Illinois: "The two bank presidents . . . talk about farmers as if they were business partners and mutual allies under attack by the rest of the Nation's economic interests." Lyford continues: "Vandalia shapes its commercial activities to suit the farmer's tastes, and the farmer, his wife and children, and his trucks are a regular part of the scenery on Gallatin Street. This is not to say that the town has been taken over by farmers: in one sense it is the farmers who have changed their habits and tastes—even in dress—to fit the town."[29]

The 1920s was a period of renewed boosterism. "Boards of Trade,"

Farm wife returned from shopping at Villa Grove, Illinois (1928). The automobile enabled farm families to spend more time in town. The dress and manners of most farm families became indistinguishable from that of people in town. Country folk increasingly thought themselves part of town-focused communities.

"Commercial Clubs," and "Chambers of Commerce" in the larger towns renewed efforts to attract industry, hoping to build more diversified economies on the enlarged retail markets captured with the arrival of the automobile. W. L. White writes sarcastically of the town promoter: "It was pleasant in the middle twenties to be a . . . progressive, to look ahead through a golden haze into the future, seeing it (as every generation must) as an enlarged and ennobled projection of the past—looking up a never-ending causeway of progress which was composed of orderly little steps."[30] But the period's idealism, optimism, and abiding faith in progress was short-lived. Towns could not compete with the cities for industrial jobs. The automobile brought only transition to the small town, not progress in the sense of growth and maturation. Boosterism brought disillusionment to most places. Disappointment, in turn, brought lethargy as the Depression set in.

Through the 1930s small-town people were more fully integrated into the urban mainstream of American life. Small towners adopted big-city values more fully. They clamored after technological innovations in automobiles, appliances, radios, and sundry other products mass-produced in the cities and advertised in the city dominated media. Art Gallaher writes of "Plainville" after World War II:

> Suddenly . . . the community was caught up in a postwar "revolution of expectations" from which it has never recovered. The people of Plainville . . . daily feel the impact of accelerated postwar American advertising, which turns novelties into necessities, and they, and the rest of America, daily sense the productive might of a war-fattened industry, hungry for peacetime consumer markets, which makes yesterday's purchases obsolete today. Little wonder that technology is a dominant concern and that Plainvillers' interest now focuses sharply in technological change.[31]

New technology costs more in the small town. Small-town factories did not enjoy the same economies of large-scale production as in the cities, nor did small-town merchants do business in large volumes. Small towns had less access to fabricated materials and markets, and costs of doing business were higher excepting labor costs. Consumer prices remained high and incomes low.

America's small towns changed greatly in economy, orientation to work, attitudes toward money, and use of leisure time. But underlying all of these changes was the pervasive belief in the inevitability of change itself. If one did not have change for the better, then one had change for the worse: if not growth, then decline. Things did not, could not, stay the same. In many small towns of the 1940s and 1950s a sense of helplessness promoted the status quo in preference to losing more money, time, and emotional energy in boosterism. The institutions for managing economic change faltered. Many small towns lost their sense of progress completely.

The small town could not continue to occupy its traditional niche in the American economy. Opinions differed as to just what that niche had been, but people seemed to agree that the new metropolitan orientation in American life called for less concern with small places. Many commentators predicted the small town's demise as a viable economic form. Geographer Peirce Lewis sampled books and articles indicative of this prevalent mid–twentieth century view: "A Town that has Gone Downhill" (1927)," "Villages Are Dying—And Who Cares?" (1931), "Is the Small Town Doomed?" (1944), "The Passing of the American Village" (1952), "Can Our Small Towns Survive?" (1960), and "Is Main Street Still There?" (1970)[32]

The Look of Downtown

The automobile's impact on the small town was apparent downtown. Streets were widened and resurfaced with concrete or asphalt. Hitching posts, watering troughs, and other obstructions to automobile traffic were removed. Storefronts at both ends of Main Street were converted to automobile sales and/or service. Harness, carriage, and blacksmith shops reoriented to automobile-related customers or went out of business. Livery stables and feed and sales barns became garages. Just beyond the

Garage, town unknown (1920). Livery stables, blacksmith shops, and other horse-related business buildings were reoriented to the automobile. Garages were also created out of storefronts, especially on the side streets off Main Street.

business district, certain corner lots were cleared of houses and gasoline stations were erected. Carole Rifkind in *Main Street* summarizes: "The . . . automobile's appetite for road space, parking space, and service space was insatiable. The auto monopolized the curb, encroached on the site of the demolished town hall . . . and usurped the central square. Parking lot and service station bit into the town fabric, digesting corners, gouging holes in street fronts and devouring those intricate relationships that hold a city together.[33]

The courthouse was usually a county seat's centerpiece and its biggest single generator of traffic. Businesses sought to locate as near it as possible. Parking space was usually in short supply. J. B. Jackson writes of "Optimo City," Oklahoma:

> The Court House itself attracts so many out of town visitors that the problem of parking is acute. The only solution that occurs to the enlightened minds of the Chamber of Commerce is to tear the Court House down, use the place for parking, and build a new one somewhere else. They have already had an architect draw a sketch of a new court house to go at the far end of Main Street; a chaste concrete cube . . . a fine specimen of Bureaucrat Modernism.[34]

Courthouses on diamond squares interrupted the vistas up and down Main Street and the main cross street. In Jackson's "Optimo City," the courthouse interrupted the flow of traffic coming and going in all four directions, resulting in a sluggish eddy of vehicles and pedestrians.

> Saturday, of course, is the best day for seeing the full tide of human existence. . . . The rows of parked pickups are like cattle in a feed lot; the sidewalks in front of . . . the Mercantile, the Ranch Cafe, Sears, the drugstore, resound to the mincing steps of cowboy boots; farmers and ranchers, thumbs in their pants pockets, gather in groups to lament the drought (there is always a drought) . . . while their wives go from store to movie house to store. Radios, juke-boxes, the bell in the courthouse tower; the teenagers doing "shave-and-a-haircut; bay rum" on the horns of their parents' cars as they drive round and round the square.[35]

Downtown streets were painted with stripes to mark parking spaces; signs regulating parking and traffic appeared. Angle parking was most popular in the 1930s and 1940s—cars angled in at the curbs and often at the diagonal down the very center of Main Street. In Homer Croy's "Junction City":

> An irregular line of automobiles stood in the middle of the street, where once ox teams switched their tails and fought flies. In the mid-

dle of the street, on the four corners surrounding ''the square,'' were barrels filled with cement, and in them were iron standards which said, ''Go slowly,'' ''Keep to the Right,'' and strung around the barrels were painted signs of home-made construction which said, ''No Jay Walking Allowed.''[36]

Square at Washington, Iowa (1935). Washington's square nicely accommodated the automobile. Local merchants appeared prosperous, with renovated storefronts across the lower stories of their buildings. The chain store had made its appearance.

Through such contrivances Main Street was converted from a space for pedestrians to one for machines.

Merchants sought to ''modernize'' Main Street, and town governments bent to their will more often than not. Trees planted along the street did not symbolize progress. Theodore Dreiser writes of Carmel, Indiana:

> Once there had been trees, beautiful ones, but with the arrival of the metropolitan spirit and a desire to catch passing automobile trade it was decided to widen the street somewhat and make it more commercial and therefore more attractive . . . the trees should come down. ''Why?'' asked some lover of the trees as things of beauty. ''Well, you don't see any trees in Main Street, Indianapolis, do you?'' replied another triumphantly. The battle was lost and won right there—Main Street, Indianapolis, was the criterion.[37]

After the First World War the new buildings that appeared along American Main Streets were plain and nondescript—utility increasingly squeezed aesthetics aside in the merchant's attempt to look up-to-date.

129

Peirce Lewis writes of Bellefonte, Pennsylvania's legacy of late nineteenth and early twentieth century architecture. Many good neo-Romanesque buildings had been built in Bellefonte, and the town had more than its share of Richardsonian buildings, but there was "not a single example of distinguished post-1920 architecture anywhere in the business district."[38] "Form followed function" and "less was more" in the new modern era.

New building materials began to appear on storefronts, not only on new buildings but on old renovated structures where lower stories were altered to conform to the times. Terra-cotta and other forms of tile were common, especially in the larger towns of the Midwest and West. Commerce Street in Longview, Texas, took on a modern scrubbed look. Not only were the street and sidewalks paved and new streetlights installed in Longview, but power poles and trees were removed and angle parking instituted. Above all, two new department stores faced in terra-cotta were built at the town's principal intersection. The clean lines of the buildings reflected the clean aspect of the street. Architectural decoration on the two stores was reduced to small patterns of tile banded in layers to emphasize the horizontal rather than the vertical dimensions of the buildings. Narrow, confined storefronts were replaced in popularity by expanses of large display windows strung along wide storefronts.

Business district at Longview, Texas (circa 1930). Merchants sought to establish a clean, antiseptic image with new buildings and storefront renovations after World War I. The new look symbolized the new era of advanced technology epitomized by the automobile.

Plainness in architecture was promoted by the chain stores which built simple, undecorated facades to contrast with older surrounding buildings. The Montgomery Ward store in Woodstock, Illinois, clearly stood out not only for its size, but for its plain front—which contrasted with the red brick and frilly detailing of traditional stores. The chain stores

Square at Woodstock, Illinois (1941). New storefronts contrasted sharply with older, nearby buildings, thus calling maximum attention to the ''modern'' businesses within. Storefront renovation tended to break up the continuity of older Main Street blocks. Business self-interest diminished Main Street's value as a symbol of community integration.

Business district at Eagle River, Wisconsin (1938). Electric signs coupled with holiday decorations provided a colorful nighttime aspect previously unknown on Main Street.

used large signs standardized from town to town to create brand and company identities. Large neon and other electric signs helped to light Main Street at night. Electric signs suspended over the sidewalks sought to attract the passing motorist, now a more important customer than the pedestrian.

Merchants devoted more and more of their storefronts to signs. Each sought to make a loud and distinctive pitch to prospective customers, irrespective of the disruption to the business blocks which had previously made Main Street seem architecturally integrated. Curtin Bolivar, the father of Quince, walked the streets of Mary King's fictional "Good Union," Oklahoma: "He came to a garage. 'Hot Shot Motor Hospital. You Wreck 'Em We Fix 'Em.' The front of the garage and the gasoline pumps were bright orange. The workshop and the living quarters above had been given a prize coat of aluminum paint that glittered like steel in the morning sun."[39]

State Bank at Fremont, Michigan (1925). Bankers substantially influenced the look of Main Street. Not only did they set style changes in the remodeling of bank buildings, but their tastes affected mortgage holders and loan applicants in search of remodeling money for Main Street's other buildings.

Banks were usually remodeled with more class. They still had to symbolize strength and security, business characteristics increasingly important after the stock market crash of 1929. Not only were banks style setters in small-town architecture, but bankers—as holders of the town's purse strings—influenced how other buildings would look. W. L. White writes of fictional "Athena":

> In the spring of 1929 five chain stores and three Athena banks an-
> nounced remodeling plans—new fronts, new fixtures, new everything!
> The Athena First National's building, on the busiest corner of Main
> Street, was of course the best remodeling job. The front was simply
> gray stone, clean modern lines, with the bank's name in big bronze let-
> ters. The old iron grille cages had been cleared away, and you were
> separated from the bank's officers only by a low marble railing—there
> they were in plain view, sitting at the slickest new mahogany desks you
> ever saw![40]

At those desks "Athena's" bankers decided which merchants and which
property owners would receive remodeling money, and how that money
was to be spent.

Next to bankers, lawyers probably exerted the greatest influence on
how downtown looked. Charles Givens writes of fictional "Tirus" and
the new Professional Building as "a gaudy pile of gray stone and shiny
marble . . . among the grimy-gray frame buildings surrounding it." It
housed the town's up-and-coming lawyers, the sons of the oldsters who
had been content to have their offices in little white cottages along the
back of the courthouse square.

> The sons of the old ones were all down in the spanking new Profes-
> sional Building, starving to death in grandeur and shouting for a big-
> ger and better Tirus; howling and bawling for sewers, for paved
> streets, for a new electric light and water plant, beating the tom-toms
> of progress in the vain hope that some out-of-town labor usurer would
> . . . erect a chair factory, a canning plant, or . . . a hosiery mill.[41]

Lawyers sought public office and careers in politics. They used their
knowledge of the law to amass property, and their political connections to
enhance the value of that property. Next to bankers, lawyers had the inside track on a town's real estate.

Among the new buildings which appeared along America's Main
Street, the movie theaters were the most glamorous. The movie theater
was a place to escape the humdrum realities of small-town life. The Liberty Theater was showing *Action in Arabia* the day the accompanying
photograph was taken. The building's facade was little more than two
gigantic signs trimmed in tile. The theater gleamed in the sun by day, and
glittered in the reflected neon by night. Many theater managers played action films in the summer when country audiences were large. The movie
show was a place for farm families to cool off in hot weather, as well as a
place to be entertained. Society films were shown during the winter when
town people dominated movie audiences.[42] On Saturday afternoons the
show was filled with children come to see Tom Mix, Tarzan, Flash Gor-

133

don, and their successors.

By 1960 only a few older business buildings were unchanged both inside and out. Sill's Cafe in Larry Woiwode's fictional "Hyatt," North Dakota, was such a place. The cafe's facade of counterfeit orange brick shingle had been lounged against so much that the bricks were rubbed away to disclose the underlying asphalt. Inside there were "Marbled topped [sic] tables and metal ice-cream chairs, a counter with swivel stools, a row of comfortable booths along one wall . . . and a glass display case that contained everything from wristwatches to licorice to home made cupcakes, cap guns, and jawbreakers." Suspended from long pipes attached to the stamped-metal ceiling were wood-bladed fans, which spun to activate streamers of paper intended to frighten away flies.[43] Each year there were fewer reminders of the old Main Street left.

Motion picture theater at Libertyville, Illinois (circa 1955). Long had false fronts maximized the visual impact of front facades on Main Street, while minimizing overall structural costs. The Liberty Theater facade was little more than an integrated marquee and sign. A walk down any back alley revealed that cheaper materials and less careful craftsmanship typified the backs of most Main Street buildings.

Main Street was dominated more by machines. In Hamilton Basso's "Macedon," South Carolina:

A loudspeaker, suspended above the entrance of Zeke Kingston's plumbing and electrical supply store, competed with the phonograph in the door of the five-and-ten. . . . Negroes lounged on the street corners, murmurous, breaking into laughter, and in the reddish glow of Murphy's neon sign the town's young blades stood huddled like a

134

football squad, eyeing and chiding the girls. . . . In the ticket booth of
the motion picture theater, the rush for the first show over, Miss Jane
Tucker sat rouged and blond and absorbed—reading a total confes-
sion of surrender and regret.[44]

The noise of automobiles and trucks dominated "Macedon," especially in
the busy hours. The smell of exhaust fumes was evident in the streets and
sometimes in the stores although, as the automobile replaced the horse,
less manure decorated the streets and fewer flies were apparent.

Prohibition brought changes to Main Street. When the saloons
closed, soda fountains and pool halls throve. Pool halls continued to be
places for general congregation and relaxation for men and boys. The
churchgoing middle class of America's small towns had been among the
staunchest supporters of the Volstead Act. This support was, in part, a
reaction to immigrant populations which had crowded many of the mill
and mining towns, and which had infiltrated many farming communities.
Taverns and saloons served as social clubs for many minority groups.
With Prohibition the enemy merely withdrew to reform its lines. As W. L.
White writes: "The same rugged sour-faced people from below the tracks
who once thronged saloons now frequented pool halls."[45] In "Plainville"
the pool room was called "a hall of sin" and the owner was accused of
"leading them young boys astray" and "having a bad influence on the
menfolks."[46] The gentry impulse fought the pool halls in various ways:
progressive people "erected civic centers of Y.M.C.A.'s where boys might
come to play basketball or swim in the tiled pool, where scout masters
taught the children of the poor to love nature, to identify the whistles of
various birds, and the art of tying knots in ropes."[47]

Accommodating the Car at Home

Residential landscapes were also changed by the automobile. The
business districts in larger towns expanded along adjacent residential
streets—streets widened to accommodate more automobiles. Increased
traffic hastened the conversion of residential properties to commercial
uses. As a business district expanded, a zone of transition was created. As
seen in the oblique aerial photograph of Tomahawk, Wisconsin, in the
1940s, various streets had been widened for angle parking. Trees had been
removed. Business buildings had been built where houses had stood
before. Many of these businesses were garages, or otherwise catered
directly to automobile sales or service.

Residential and commercial properties no longer mixed neatly in
many towns. Parking lots, and vacant lots held in anticipation of commercial development, gave the margins of downtown a ragged appearance.
Houses near downtown were no longer owner occupied, but were rented

out and therefore poorly maintained. The largest houses were divided into rental units or were occupied by businesses such as funeral homes. In 1916 Theodore Dreiser was shocked to see Warsaw, Indiana's largest mansion houses where forty years before the town's elite had lived: an automobile agency occupied one structure, and the porch was crowded with tires and posters advertising the latest car models; another house served as a lodge hall.[48]

Aerial view of Tomahawk, Wisconsin (1941). Business had intruded onto residential streets adjacent to the business district. The smooth transition between the business district and surrounding residential space had been disrupted through accommodation of the automobile. Few small towns were known from their aerial perspective; postcards with bird's-eye views were not best-sellers.

Change did not come everywhere. In Sac City, Iowa, Main Street had not been widened and the trees had not been removed even though the street was a well-travelled federal highway. Only one gasoline station anchored the business end of Main Street, where the gentry still lived. Here the institutional buffer of several churches and the public library, which still protected residential properties from commercial speculation, enabled Sac City's residential show street to survive.

Residential streets were improved in "progressive" towns. The brick pavements of the 1920s were widened with narrow strips of concrete and new curbs in the 1930s or 1940s. In the 1950s whole streets were covered with asphalt. Sometimes new water mains and sewers accompanied street improvements but, as often as not, the new streets of one year were ripped up for other kinds of improvement another year. New water mains brought fire hydrants and, in the larger towns, call boxes connected to the downtown fire station. The dominance of the automobile with its faster

136

Main Street at Sac City, Iowa (1949). The town's business district and its more prestigious residential sector blended smoothly along Main Street, despite the street's demarcation as a federal highway.

Main Street at Sac City, Iowa (1949). The highway brought heavy truck traffic. Dirt, noise, and the vibration of trucks substantially devalued adjacent properties for residential purposes, prompting the town's more affluent families to move to new subdivisions.

137

speeds of travel necessitated improved street lighting in residential as well as commercial areas. The single bulb swaying over the intersections of residential neighborhoods gave way to rows of evenly spaced light standards.

Stables and other outbuildings were converted to automobile storage, or torn down in favor of new garages. As the automobile had greatly stimulated the money economy at the expense of traditional forms of barter and subsistence, hen houses, barns, woodsheds, gardens, and orchards disappeared from behind houses. Backyards were cleaned up in the more affluent neighborhoods. New driveways of gravel and concrete replaced rear alleys; automobiles were displayed with pride in front drives.

Promotion for new subdivision at Effingham, Illinois (1918). At first new subdivisions were simply extensions of existing street grids. After World War I curvilinear streets were introduced in more stylish developments, in imitation of big-city suburbs.

Residential street grids were extended in the more viable towns. In Effingham, Illinois, a new subdivision was opened in 1916. The sign on the back of the Model T shown in the photograph reads: "Free Auto To Woods Terrace." New subdivisions assumed rural, pastoral names mimicking big-city suburbs. Vacant lots in the old neighborhoods, which had previously served as pastures or gardens or had been held in speculation, were built upon. Bungalows and other new styles of houses intermixed with the older dwellings. A few new houses had attached garages—the family and its automobile sheltered under a single roof.

The automobile brought the country club to America's small towns. Located at the edge of town where open space easily accommodated a golf course, a tennis court, a swimming pool, and a clubhouse, the country

138

club was a private pleasure ground for a town's more affluent families. It could be reached only by automobile. Distance separated it from the common herd. Paul Corey describes a country club in his novel *County Seat*:

> It was a sprawling building, blanked by verandas and hedged in with snowball, bridal wreath and lilac bushes. Light from the ballroom flowed through the windows, lighting the verandas and silhouetting the couples out for a little air. The music of August Eippinger's jazz band seemed to flow with the light—the quick beat of "Yes, sir, that's my baby," the melancholy lament of "all alone, by the telephone," and the raucous pounding of "The Storm," echoed far over the greens and fairways.[49]

The country club presented a pastoral setting for a town's gentry families. Here was a deliberate turning away from the small-town pretense at social equality.

The Car and Public Facilities

Courthouse and town hall benefited from the increase of parking space downtown. Churches located just beyond downtown were not as fortunate. Sunday mornings found streets around the older churches crowded with parked automobiles. Small towners found walking increasingly demeaning and inconvenient and, like motorists everywhere, they

Church at Genoa, Illinois (1941). Fewer families walked to church on Sunday. Automobiles crowded adjacent streets, symbolizing both a congregation's general prosperity and its success as a church.

demanded parking spaces at and not near their destinations. Churches inconvenient to the automobile were thought to be less successful at attracting and retaining members. Congregations desiring growth were faced with two alternatives. Adjacent properties could be bought, houses destroyed, and parking lots created. Such churches made poor neighbors for their parking lots depressed adjacent property values, thus creating neighborhood instability. Churches could also move to vacant land at the edge of town, where large parking lots could be easily built.

High-school gymnasium at Cedarburg, Wisconsin (circa 1950). New public facilities located at or near a town's center reasserted the traditional symbolic association between centrality and sense of community.

Schools were not only faced with parking problems, but with the lack of room for expansion as well. It was a fortunate community that found adequate space for a new gymnasium next to the old high-school building. School consolidation necessitated large structures. After World War II tastes in new school buildings, even additions to old buildings, ran to spread-out, single-story complexes. Many towns moved their schools to the edge of town and relied on school buses to move not only rural children, but town children as well. Even the journey to school required an automobile or its equivalent.

Factories in the Automobile Age

The automobile helped solidify a mass market for machine-made products, much to the detriment of local artisans. Craftsmen had flourished in the relative isolation of the horse and wagon era, when the national economy was less specialized.[50] Most towns had a range of small-scale manufacturers—gunsmiths, coopers, blacksmiths, tanners, cigar makers, broom makers. Not only were their products handmade, but often the tools were, too. But in "Plainville" of the 1940s, nearly all tools and machines in use were manufactured. "There are no local wagon builders or coffin makers any more. No one makes ax handles or wagon tongues, few do their own shoe cobbling, few repair any broken tool or implement beyond 'just fixin' her up with bailin' wire and lettin' 'er go.'"[51]

When machine-produced merchandise flooded small-town markets, many local artisans had turned to retailing. The watch and clock makers opened jewelry stores, their earlier craftsmanship finding an outlet in the repairing of watches and the fitting of eyeglasses.[52] Tailors turned to selling factory-made suits in men's stores. Blacksmith shops were converted to garages and welding shops. Machine-made merchandise was not only cheaper but, because of its standardized qualities, was considered better. Local crafts and craftsmen were viewed increasingly as second-rate and redundant.

Every town hoped to have at least one factory—a means of specializing in order to reach a regional or national market with a product of its own. A local manufacturing plant selling its produce elsewhere was seen to bring money into a community in the form of wages and, if the plant was locally owned, in the form of profits. To secure a factory, and even to keep one, many towns offered substantial subsidies. In 1957 the town of Vandalia, Illinois, raised $77,000 to build a replacement plant for a shoe manufacturer who threatened to close his antiquated local facility. The town's two banks were among the largest contributors. Members of the Boot and Shoe Workers Union contributed $12,000 out of their paychecks. In 1954, Vandalians had raised $32,000 to subsidize a local factory for an outboard motor manufacturer, and in 1949 $107,000 to attract a sewing machine company with a new building.[53] The latter firm stayed only a few years, breaking its lease and paying only for upkeep and insurance on the building during its stay. Towns which successfully attracted a factory often found their roads, schools, sewers, and water system overtaxed by the new population attracted. New factories also created social tensions between new people and old.

Locally owned companies were considered more sensitive to the needs of the local community. Owners tended to be more benevolent, at least as they understood benevolence. The absentee corporation was often something else: "The local labor force [could] be exploited quite mercilessly (for it was the prospect of such exploitation which had attracted many industries in the first place), while the townspeople, anxious at any cost to retain the factory as a prized source of revenue, brought severe and sometimes brutal pressures to bear to prevent any action that might im-

Factory at Woodstock, Illinois (1941). By World War II, the relative success of larger towns east from the Great Plains and in parts of California and the Pacific Northwest was based largely on industrial jobs in small factories.

Factory at Algoma, Wisconsin (1955). After World War I industry preferred the edge of town, where land was cheap and plants could spread out with space for future expansion. The automobile made such facilities accessible to large numbers of workers. At Algoma employees traditionally walked to the mill from adjacent residential tracts.

peril the dearly bought industry.''[54] Cheap labor was usually the small town's only attraction to the industrialist besides the subsidies which a community might offer. Surplus farm labor was usually sought—people willing to commute from nearby farms or move to town altogether.

After World War I a new kind of factory building appeared in the small town landscape. Single-story structures spread out over large areas with production organized on one level, and with power distributed by electricity. Large open tracts of inexpensive land along the railroad, but at the edge of town, were preferred to congested, more expensive central locations. Workers commuted to work by automobile. The plywood mill at Algoma, Wisconsin, typified an older plant expanded in the new factory style.

The town factory, no matter how modern, symbolized a sort of alienation in small-town novels. A factory might be in a town, but somehow it was not part of the town. In *The Portion of Labor,* Mary Wilkins's child heroine, Ellen Brewster, runs away from home into the night. The factory was the most alien and frightening place for the little girl to go—the antipode of home with its security and kindness: ''Tonight when Ellen passed in her strange flight, the factories were still, though they were yet blazing with light. The gigantic buildings, after a style of architecture as simple as a child's block house, and adapted to as primitive an end, loomed up beside the road like windowed shells enclosing massive concreteness of golden light.''[55] Factories were not rooted in the town, but depended on events outside the community. Their business was not always understood by the townspeople. Often a factory's operation depended upon dominating and manipulating the town as a source of labor and capital.

The New Age of Technology

The automobile, although the most important influence on a town's changing geography, was not the only influential innovation. America entered the air age in the early twentieth century. Like the automobile the airplane was at first a novelty, crowd pleaser, and toy for wealthy enthusiasts. Towns sought to identify with the airplane as a symbol of progress. Postcard photographers early reinforced this association with trick shots of Main Street which pretended that the airplane was an integral part of the small-town scene. Orion, Michigan, still had kerosene street lamps and horses still dominated Main Street when the accompanying photograph was taken.

Private airfields began to appear in the 1920s at the edges of many towns. Fields featured grass landing strips, and sometimes shedlike hangars. A town might paint its name on the water tower, the roof of the railroad station, or on the top of some other large building such as a

Main Street at Orion, Michigan (1914). New technology symbolized progress. The photographer's car sits at the curb, the only motorized vehicle in Main Street until the airplane was superimposed on the photograph in the printing process.

Airport at Huron, South Dakota (1947). Airports subsidized by local governments had appeared outside most large towns by the 1950s. Hangars and other structures accumulated near the runways, each building reflecting a different stage in the evolution of the field if not of aviation itself. Airports were used by only a small proportion of a town's population even where scheduled airline service was available. Nonetheless, its promise for increased connection to the outside world affected all as a symbol of local progress.

lumberyard warehouse. Towns sought to locate themselves on pilots' maps. In the West, monograms began to appear on hill and mountain slopes above Main Street—"G" for Gregory, South Dakota, for example. Most of the largest towns (certainly those with a population of around ten thousand) managed to support improved airports after World War II, with improved landing strips and terminal buildings. Both world wars vastly enhanced aviation's popularity. The number of pilots increased geometrically, many trained by the army and navy. William Faulkner used both the airplane and the automobile to symbolize his characters socially and temporally. The Sartoris family epitomized the gentry of "Jefferson," Mississippi.[56] Col. John Sartoris built the railroad, Young Bayard came home by train from the war, Old Bayard lost his life in an automobile driven by Young Bayard, and Young Bayard died in an airplane crash.[57] Small-town aviation remained largely a hobby for the well-to-do businessman except where crop dusting, spraying, seeding, and other agricultural applications predominated.

Marvels of the new technological age included the electric light, the telephone, the radio and later the television. All had a profound effect on the way in which small-town people perceived their towns as places. No town could possibly consider itself up-to-date without electricity. But it was surprising how slowly electricity was adopted in many places, and how rapidly and completely it was diffused later on. As late as 1940, only two-thirds of the houses in "Plainville" had "lights."[58] The remaining houses and the bulk of the farmhouses in the area used kerosene. In 1955 all of "Plainville's" houses had electricity, and practically every kitchen had several of the following: refrigerator, washer, dryer, home freezer, mixer, toaster, range, hot-water heater, electric iron.[59] Every farm around "Plainville" had been supplied with electric power through the federally financed Rural Electrification Administration.

The telephone spread even less rapidly and less completely through small-town America. At first a town's manually operated switchboard connected the more viable businesses, governmental and professional offices, and a town's more affluent families. The telephone reduced the need for trips downtown and kept people better informed and connected. Housewives had only to call downtown and groceries were delivered directly. Emergencies could be reported promptly, and aid was quicker in coming. Smalltown gossips, who traditionally functioned over backyard fences, found telephone party lines much to their liking. The switchboard operator, and not the postmaster, was now considered the best-informed person in town.

The radio's impact was more subtle. Few small towns had radio stations of their own until after World War II. WDZ in Tuscola, Illinois, was one of the exceptions. The owner of the town's grain elevator used the radio in preference to the telephone to report grain prices to local farmers.

Jim Day

The periods between hourly price quotations were filled with music, some locally originated. When small towners listened to the radio in the 1930s and 1940s they almost always tuned in to big-city stations. The same was true of television later. Much of the programming was network originated, coming from a relatively few metropolises such as New York, Chicago, and Los Angeles.

Much of a town's casual conversation came to be radio related. In "Plainville" radio weather forecasts were closely followed. They replaced interest in the predictions of local prognosticators. People frequently asked: "Have you heard the radio? What's the news? What is the market like?"[60] Television came to most towns in the 1950s. One early owner in "Plainville" recalled that his small living room was crowded with curious neighbors "every night for a week." At first the reception was poor ("the snow was so bad it made your eyes water"), and few people thought there would be much future for television in towns remote from the big cities. But by 1955 40 percent of "Plainville's" families and 15 percent of the area's farm families owned sets.[61] People used expensive aerials and gadgets for rotating the antennas to improve reception. Small towns were known for the very tall television aerials atop the houses.

146

Conclusion

The automobile and the other technological developments of the early twentieth century profoundly affected the small town. Increased geographical mobility loosened traditional social ties. Automobile ownership, as it forced increased reliance on the money economy, encouraged new attitudes toward work. Community orientation weakened as a sense of individual self-interest grew. Geography shrank, for places were no longer as distant in terms of time. Smaller towns lost retail trade to the larger places. Main Street changed to accommodate the automobile. Towns changed from pedestrian places oriented to the railroad, to automobile places oriented to the highway.

Change in the small town, as significant and widespread as it was, seemed less consequential than what was occurring in nearby cities. If the automobile enabled the larger towns to capture the trade of smaller centers, it also diverted commerce farther up the urban hierarchy. The cities were the more successful competitors in the more integrated and highly specialized national economy. Cities dominated the media, especially advertising. Brand-name merchandise and chain stores brought small-town America into the big-city retail fold. Industry was more successful in the cities through economies of scale and access to market. More jobs at higher salaries were located there. As farmers sought jobs in the towns, so townspeople sought jobs in the cities. The city represented big growth and thus big opportunities. The small town represented slow growth (at best) and stability. Small towns meant lower incomes and more restricted prospects for the future. No matter how people compared their towns to cities, small towns usually seemed second-best.

Although many people cherished their towns as friendly communities in contrast to the impersonal cities, the onus of small-town parochialism had not entirely worn off. Intensive neighboring bred of the proverbial small-town gossip still had its negative as well as positive implications. If small towners believed their culture to be superior to big-city or cosmopolitan varieties, they did not display it in their townscapes. Landscape innovations of the cities were adopted not only because they promised technological efficiency, but simply because they were of the city. If big-city downtowns had little decorative landscaping, then the trees were torn down on Main Street to compete and conform. If big-city merchants built shiny storefronts of tile and glass, then Main Street merchants followed suit. If big-city churches had parking lots, then so did small-town churches. The small town, irrespective of its professed values, obviously aped the city. New icons defined small towns as places.

Small-town photography recorded some of the changes brought by the automobile. Albums included pictures of cars as if the cars themselves were members of the family. Commercial photographers found it

147

necessary to rephotograph Main Street at regular intervals to keep up with the improvements in street lighting, parking, signs, and storefronts—not to mention the look of the automobiles themselves. A few novelists found it necessary to embrace the automobile, not only to make their novels appear up-to-date, but—more important—to treat the impending social revolution implicit in increased geographical mobility. It was the social scientist, however, who best documented the change of pace and orientation in small-town life. The development of community case studies in the 1920s and 1930s coincided nicely with the automobile's preliminary impact on small-town life.

Seven

The Highway and Small Towns

The state asked the town to move the [Civil War] monument over a few feet so that the new paved highway would not have to jog around it. It was a hotly debated issue. Much mumbling about dictatorship by state bureaucrats. But at one of the best attended town meetings ever, the people voted to move the monument. First Selectman Fred Johnson said they had made a wise decision: "Future generations will rise up and call them blessed."
  Donald Connery, *One American Town*

Twenty-six million motor vehicles had been registered in the United States by 1930, and half a million miles of surfaced rural highways, twice the then existing railroad mileage, had been completed.[1] By 1960 the number of vehicles had increased 2½ fold, and the number of miles paved over fourfold. Highways more fully connected small towns with the outside world, diverting people to shopping, jobs, and even homes in the city. Highway improvements disrupted and sometimes critically damaged a town's landscape. Main Street was congested with highway traffic. Residential streets were converted to commerce. At a town's edge the highway evolved as a commercial strip, and in many towns Main Street declined in favor of new highway-oriented commerce. Eventually, new subdivisions sprouted in the larger, more viable places. A highway-oriented landscape came to dominate small-town America.

The Highway

The highway was as significant to towns after World War I as the railroad and the courthouse had been before. Small towns made heroic efforts to secure highway improvements, for through traffic promised additional business, and increased accessibility meant that a town could compete more successfully with other centers for surrounding farm trade. Homer Croy's fictional town of "Junction City," Missouri, was determined to be on a major road. After the highway engineers had made their survey, the state commissioners visited the town before making a decision.

149

Enthusiasms in Junction City rose. The town must be shown off at its best. Committees were formed; opposition parties joined; animosities were forgotten. There were clean-up campaigns [and] weed mowing contests; graders appeared on the streets; holes were filled in; unsightly lots were cleared off; discarded buggies, carts, crippled sleighs, broken down milkwagons, and abandoned drays were hauled to the blacksmith shop, the iron taken off, and the wood sold; the water wagons were painted . . . sweepers started down the vitrified-brick paving; there were banquets, speech making, parades, tag days, auctions, church fairs, suppers, veiled queens—the mayor put on a pair of overalls and himself cleaned up a block. The commissioners arrived; automobiles emptied themselves and distinguished-looking gentlemen walked about the town, visited the hotels, sampled the meals, examined the garages and the filling station, studied the grade books, but there was doubt. The commissioners were divided. At last they went away and Junction City waited in feverish anxiety.[2]

The novel's principal character, Guy Plummer, becomes the town's savior. Indiscretions, ten years previously, had made Guy a social outcast. But the victim of small-town gossip rises to lift the community from its provincialism. Guy travels by train to the big city, persuades the commissioners to make ''Junction City'' a highway town, and thereby wins back social respectability.

The new rural highways, paved in concrete, sped travellers from city to city and from town to town. Fewer people travelled on the railroads, preferring the comfort and convenience of their own cars. Salesmen took to automobiles. Families on tour or travelling to visit relatives filled the

U.S. 50 in West Virginia (circa 1935). Towns lobbied vigorously to be included on hard-surfaced highways. Failure to obtain a highway was as disastrous for a town in the twentieth century as failure to obtain a courthouse or railroad had been earlier.

highways, as a new culture of travel slowly evolved to focus on the automobile. Farm produce moved to market by truck, and long-distance hauling between cities became a way of life for a new breed of teamsters.

Bridge at Hannibal, Missouri (circa 1940). Mark Twain immortalized Hannibal as a river town—the Mississippi River its primary connection to the outside world. But with railroads and highways Hannibal, like other river towns, thrived primarily as a crossing point—the river a barrier funnelling overland traffic across its bridges.

In the 1920s and 1930s highway engineers in most states were preoccupied with improving existing rural roads to connect the peripheries of towns and cities. Existing streets within towns were used wherever possible. In Hannibal, Missouri, traffic from the new highway bridge flowed onto streets and into neighborhoods ill prepared to receive the flood. Often a town's prime residential street was chosen. It was wide and already paved, and it usually gave direct access to downtown. House lots were large and thus conducive to automobile-oriented commercial conversions. Lack of zoning or other land-use controls, and the small-town ethic that "a man can use his property as he pleases" hastened the conversion of residential streets into commercial strips. When the highway was routed down Main Street, business tended to spread along the thoroughfare outward from the business district, as in Benson, Arizona.

Although the process of highway orientation was slow, often requiring decades, the final results were usually devastating to those who remembered how towns had been. Donald Connery summarizes the situation in *One American Town*:

It is a town that has lost its innocence. More bluntly; which has allowed itself to be raped. Years and years of cranky resistance by a

151

Business district at Benson, Arizona (1948). Highway traffic stimulated commercial development along major thoroughfares. In Benson a motel, several gasoline stations, and several restaurants dominated the principal street.

steadily diminishing majority of the townspeople to simple zoning regulations (''Nobody's going to tell me what I can do with my land'') have left the green acres wide open to haphazard and sometimes jerry-built development. A mess has been made of some portions of the town, a long stretch of the main highway has been turned into a third-rate Sunset Strip. The contagion of ugliness has spread so that even on the handsome village green a stately old house will be pulled down with hardly a whimper of protest. . . . When some delinquent youngsters tore up parts of the village's venerable bandstand recently, it was only a sad echo of a different kind of vandalism committed and sanctioned by their elders.[3]

In towns where highways ran in residential areas, houses were converted to tourist homes or to other business uses, torn down for gasoline stations, or replaced by stores with adjacent parking lots. Others stood as residential relics converted to apartments or rooming houses. Peirce Lewis writes of the serious damage inflicted by highway improvements in Bellefonte, Pennsylvania. Streets were widened and repaved. Trees were cut down. Traffic moved faster and more noisily, and the undistinguished houses were cruelly exposed to full view. ''What had previously been pleasant residential streets have become truck highways, bringing no measurable improvement of the town's economy, and certainly not of its environmental quality. Many Bellefontonians are pleased, however, since the state paid the bill for the new pavement—not the town.''[4] Sherwood Anderson romanticizes the highway reluctantly. He writes of ''streams of cars always flowing through the towns, endless rivers of cars, American

152

restlessness. . . . On summer nights as you lie on your bed in your house in the American town, you hear the heavy rumble of goods trucks.''[5]

The highway at the town's edge was ripe for commercial development. Gasoline stations, motels, restaurants, and transitory businesses oriented to travellers, such as fruit and vegetable stands, dominated small-town roadsides until after World War II. In ''Plainville'':

> The immediate effect was to make roughly one-fourth of the village businesses directly dependent on ''outsiders'' who travel the highway. These firms are attuned to such business and regulate their activities and ethics accordingly. They maintain longer hours, advertise with neon signs, and cater to tourists and travelers. The latter are expected to pay more than local customers, particularly for automotive goods and services, and, in fact, they do—two cents more per gallon for gasoline, and those unfortunate enough to have mechanical difficulties are charged more for repair services than hometowners.[6]

Many Main Street businesses moved to peripheral highway locations. Often the farm equipment and automobile dealers were first, drawn by the large tracts of relatively inexpensive land for storage lots. Next came the highway service trade: gasoline stations, restaurants, and motels. Finally, the heart of Main Street's business moved—grocery, hardware, and other retail stores. Retail space on the highway was organized horizontally with sales, storage, and office areas on a single floor. Gone were the lofts and

Main Street at Wonder Lake, Illinois (1948). A new form of commercial building dominated on the highway at the edge of town, or in towns—like Wonder Lake—built after World War II. Stores were single-story structures, with large expanses of plate glass facing directly onto adjacent parking space.

basements of older buildings. Wide storefronts featured large expanses of glass which stared out on adjacent parking spaces. Buildings were utilitarian, often to the extreme.

Before World War II most highway businesses were only marginally profitable. Most buildings were built at minimal cost without architectural integrity. Americans did not expect attractive facades on the highway; they expected automobile convenience. Large electric signs and new transparent facades served to entice motorists off the highway and into parking lots, out of automobiles and into stores. Inside, stores were arranged for self-service with racks of merchandise and checkout counters. Gone were the long counters behind which clerks filled customers' orders.

Flimsily constructed buildings, minimal if any landscaping, poorly constructed driveways, and crudely crafted signs typified the small-town roadside through the 1950s. Merchants sought survival on the basis of lower land costs and the advantages of intercepting farm customers and travellers at the edge of town. Business turnover was high. The remodeling of buildings and signs was constant, giving the highway strip an unfinished, transitory appearance. The strip was spread out in contrast to the concentrated pedestrian space of the traditional Main Street. Customers needed an automobile to get from store to store.

Peripheral shopping centers appeared outside most large towns in the late 1950s and early 1960s. There stores were clustered for one-stop shopping. These businesses tended to be owned by outsiders, as J. B. Jackson writes of the Midwest: "The nearer you get to town the thicker the signs and billboards become, then service stations, trailer courts, used car lots, supermarkets and motels appear. The climax of the whole strip development is 'Towne and Country Plaza,' a stylish . . . shopping center recently built by a Chicago firm, and almost entirely tenanted by chain stores."[7] After 1960 chain stores and franchised outlets predominated on small-town highway strips. Not only did Main Street lose control of local retail markets, but whole towns found themselves dominated by outside business interests. Outsiders took advantage of laissez-faire land policies to locate businesses at will. Towns without zoning or other land-use controls could not direct commercial development. Residential streets could not be protected; Main Street with its locally owned and operated businesses could not be reinforced.

The automobile promised to be a liberator, to provide people with greater mobility. Mobility unchecked made the automobile a leveller as well. As the architect Robert Riley points out, the automobile made one town look very much like another, with the same new buildings, the same parking lots, and the same subdivisions. In addition, the automobile created its own rural sprawl, blending town and country with little houses stretching along both sides of every decent road out of town.[8] Farm land close to town, given its potential for urban development, was valued higher with accordingly higher taxes. Farmers found it expedient to sell or subdivide such land, to profit from rather than lose to inflated values. A town's anticipated spread became a self-fulfilling prophecy instrumented through the taxing system.

Subdivisions with new ranch-style houses appeared outside the larger places. No longer did towns expand by extending the grid: new subdivisions were self-contained, featuring curvilinear streets as in the suburbs of the big cities. The pastoralism of the country club hit home.

> On the outskirts of the town, in the midst of fields, a housing development. . . . A compact mass of some fifty all but identical dwellings, Meadowview Heights occupies a rigidly bounded portion of what a few years ago was a cornfield entirely flat. The development is artfully laid out along a series of curving roads, leading to no particular destination. The houses . . . still too new to have acquired individuality . . . lack gardens and all but the slimmest of trees.[9]

New highways and other improved roads encouraged school districts to relocate schools. After World War I many town and country school districts consolidated to cut operating costs and improve instruction. Inefficient rural schools were closed and farm children bused to nearby towns. After World War II smaller towns found it difficult to maintain schools without further consolidation—the joining of adjacent towns in integrated school districts, with new buildings between towns or outside a county seat. A town deprived of a functioning school lost a local payroll, a facility capable of housing a variety of community events, and the sense of identity which went with educating one's children in one's own community.

Tending to Tourists

Railroad travellers once entered the small town at its center. Located nearby was the town's best facade—its best commercial buildings, its fanciest churches, and its largest and most distinguished houses. The railroad station served as a gate of entry. Looking from the center toward the periphery, the small town was reasonably ordered and attractive. But the highway turned the old order around. Visitors who came by automobile first encountered a town's periphery, where business had expanded outward in haphazard fashion. The highway approach to most towns lacked clear identity. The proliferation of billboards and other signs along the highway only obscured efforts by local chambers of commerce or by local social clubs to erect signs marking a town's entrance—to direct visitors to the next meeting of the Rotary Club, or invite investment in a new factory.

The small town roadside did not evolve at once. It resulted from a myriad of individual decisions: property owners deciding to sell, speculators deciding to buy, businessmen deciding to orient themselves to new ways of merchandising. New kinds of highway-oriented enterprises evolved, such as the tourist home and the motel. At first the downtown hotels served the automobile trade, but hotels without parking facilities were inconvenient for the traveler who arrived by car. In the East, tourist homes sprouted where the highway approached downtown, especially during the Depression. Sherwood Anderson writes: "The man who once owned the town hardware store or who is a cashier in the town bank and went broke in '29, still owns a big brick house. There is a sign in the street before his house. 'Tourist Home' the sign says."[10] In the West, the automobile camp made its appearance just outside of town. Campgrounds, public and private, were set aside where motorists could pitch their tents. Water, firewood, and toilet and shower facilities were provided. The private auto camp grew into the cabin camp when permanent structures were built; and the cabin camp became the cabin court or tourist court when cabins were winterized and provided with plumbing. "Motels" appeared as strung together cabins, integrated structures often built around crescent drives or rectangular courtyards.

Gasoline stations followed their own evolution from curbside pumps in front of downtown stores, to small houses with canopies covering pumps and driveways. After World War II oblong boxes, covered in porcelain enamel and glass or built of cinder block, typified small towns as they did the cities. Gasoline stations replaced the livery stables and other

Cottage court at Manistee, Michigan (circa 1950). Traveler-oriented businesses led the way along peripheral highways. Many motels were built unit by unit, with each year's profits plowed into expansion. Motels were vulnerable to highway relocation. The message on this postcard reads: "Name changed to Manistee Motel Court. 21 units on Old U.S. 31."

Motor court at Bridgman, Michigan (1940). The back of this advertising card claimed: ''Grande Vista. America's finest Tourist Court.'' City people came to experience small towns primarily as overnight stopping places.

Main Street at Delta, Wisconsin (1940). The most profitable businesses in many smaller towns were the traveler-oriented enterprises, especially gasoline stations and garages.

locations like the depot as gathering places for idlers. Gasoline stations had about them an air of constant activity, the constant solving of mechanical problems big and inconsequential. The gasoline station was also a place to watch travelers passing through; it was the modern small-town theater of the everyday.

Diner at Lebanon, Missouri (circa 1940). As Americans left the railroads to travel by car, the dining car, renamed the diner, followed them to the roadside.

During the 1930s old railroad cars and streetcars found their way to the highway. Converted into restaurants, they were symbolic of the nation's shift in transportation priorities. Signs on these restaurants read "Diner," or simply "Eat," and were lit in neon.[11] Theodore Dreiser writes of one diner in New York State:

> Inside was the usual "hash slinger" at his pots and pans. He had nothing to offer save pork and beans, ham and eggs, various sandwiches, and one kind of pie . . . the place was invaded by five evening roysterers, smart boys of the town, who made all sorts of quips and jests as to the limited bill of fare. "How about a whole egg? Have you got one?" "Do you ever keep any salt and pepper here, Jake?" "Somebody said you'd have a new pie, tomorrow. Is that right?"[12]

Small-town restaurant decor followed the national fads and fashions. J. B. Jackson saw little regional character in the restaurants of "Optimo City," Oklahoma, save the food: "You'll find no restaurant in town with atmosphere—no chandeliers made out of wagonwheels, no wall decorations of famous brands, no bar disguised as the Hitching Rail or the Old

158

Corral. Under a high ceiling with a two-bladed fan in the middle, you'll eat ham hock and beans, hot bread, ice tea without lemon, and like it or go without." [13]

New "highway towns" took form. George R. Stewart writes of Wendover on the Utah-Nevada line in his book, *U.S. 40: Cross Section of the United States:*

> To tourists, truckers, and bus-passengers it is the natural stopping-place—for gas, or lunch, or a cup of coffee. . . . The importance of U.S. 40 in the life of Wendover may be seen by the way in which all businesses string out along the pavement. At the foot of the hill is a small motel; then, two service stations, next, a garage; then cabins, another motel, and a third service station. The large white building on the rise . . . is the chief hotel-restaurant, the bus-stop.[14]

In such places the automobile was a necessity. "Only people who were assuming the use of automobiles would so have scattered a town," Stewart concludes.[15]

Many small towns extended their tourist industry to develop as full-fledged resort towns. Towns blessed with outstanding physical environments found it easy to attract and hold large seasonal populations. But most towns had to work hard at attracting visitors even when lakes, mountains, or other amenities were close at hand. Old resorts originally served by railroads or interurbans had to adjust to the automobile. Hotels

Resort at Hyannis, Massachusetts (1924). After World War I automobile touring became a vacation preoccupation for middle-class Americans. Resorts and resort towns accommodated the automobile or failed.

installed parking lots or went out of business. Various automobile associations published guidebooks listing the more attractive resort facilities, and signs of recommendation became common as the automobile and quality in overnight accommodations became integrally linked.

Many towns established festivals and otherwise sought to promote unique images. Small towns claiming to be a "world capital" of this or that ran epidemic from Castroville, California (the "Artichoke Capital of the World"), to West Plains, Missouri (the "Feeder Pig Capital"), to Waynesboro, Georgia (the "Bird Dog Capital"). Of course, almost every town had some claim to fame which it could advertise on the highway signs which welcomed tourists to town—"Home of the Dairy Princess," "Home of the State Basketball Champions," or, simply, "A Fine Place to Live." Where towns successfully promoted distinctive identities, tourists followed. More motels, gasoline stations, and restaurants accumulated along the highway with other businesses.

After 1956, towns located along the routes of new limited-access interstate highways felt a second highway impact. Freeway construction either bypassed a town, or concentrated tourists and other travelers at one or two interchanges. Business, which had reoriented to older highways beginning in the 1920s, found it necessary to reorient once again. Sometimes no towns existed where highways dictated that motels, gasoline

Highway at Breezewood, Pennsylvania (1964). By 1960 substantial uniformity had developed along small-town roadsides from one part of the United States to another. The large corporation, through chain and franchise stores, was more evident in the landscape—another form of the small town's big-city reorientation.

stations, and restaurants ought to be. New towns came into existence as little more than highway strips. For example, Breezewood in Pennsylvania was formed at an interchange on the Pennsylvania Turnpike.

For the majority of Americans who lived in cities, the roadside became the predominant image of small-town life. Small towns were known primarily as places to break highway travel. Few urbanites got closer to small-town America than the motel or the restaurant at the edge of town. Few lived in small towns beyond intermittent overnight stays. The Jack Kerouacs who searched America's highways for excitement completely accepted the small town as vital to extreme mobility.[16]

Automobile Leisure

The highway, which catered to the rest and relaxation of travelers, became the recreational center for local populations as well. With time, taverns, a bowling alley, drive-in restaurants, a miniature golf course, a drive-in movie, and a skating rink accumulated at the edge of the typical town. The neon glitter of the highway was too much competition for the older Main Street, at least at night. The highway became the gathering place for teenagers and young adults. Joseph Lyford writes of Vandalia, Illinois: "the substitute for something to do is for a gang to pile into a car and drive a traditional circuit in and about town, down Gallatin Street, around in the Kroger parking lot back up Gallatin Street, then out Route 51 to Route 40 to stop for a hamburger, then back to the raceway."[17]

"Cruising" became the principal pastime for a town's youth. Adults had previously "gone to town" or "gone downtown" on Friday or Saturday nights to shop and sit in their cars; but after World War II they tended to stay home in increasing numbers. Saturday night on Vandalia's strip was "a steady stream of flap-fendered vehicles, hot rods, and family sedans traveling in all directions and honking at familiar cars going in the opposite direction."[18] Cruising also filled the hours after high school let out each day. Paul Horgan writes in his novel, *Whitewater*:

> It was a familiar sight to see one or two carloads of the youth with or without their girls . . . riding around town up and down Central Avenue, it would seem, over and over again. They would pause for a root beer and drink it as they resumed riding. A favorite ride was to switch over from the bus station to . . . Highway 31. . . . They would ride out as far as Maudies' and turn around, full of talk of what went on inside the road house.[19]

The highway was the new playground. Afternoons and Saturday evenings resounded with roaring exhaust pipes, screeching tires, and honking horns.

Planning for the Automobile

The automobile and the highway affected the small town substantially. Few towns were prepared to cope with the resultant disruption to the traditional landscape. Except at their founding, when town developers exerted controlling influence over spatial organization, few towns deliberately planned for change. Change in the landscape was simply allowed to run its course. The professional planner's concern with land-use control ran counter to the typical American's deep regard for the sanctity of private property—a value amplified in small towns where a larger proportion of the population owned land, in contrast to the cities. Few towns could afford professional planners and, when hired, city-trained professionals often found it difficult to communicate with small town people. A. W. Fawcett notes that small-town government, like small-town business, involved an amateur tradition. Among small-towners "common sense is a virtue highly prized; expertness in some dimly felt way, connotes 'uppishness' in the possessor."[20]

Officials in small towns made decisions which affected friends and neighbors. They dealt personally with known people, not impersonally with strangers. Zoning or other decisions often directly affected officials and their families through an intricate web of small-town interactions. Officials might avoid decision making, or persistently uphold private interests over the more abstract community benefit. Participation in local government tended to be "risk-avoidance" in nature. In addition, many small-town officials were amateurs who donated their time to local office. They were chosen by popular election. There was no merit system, and the rate of turnover was high. Planning required an informed awareness of long-term goals and procedures, which was often lacking in the short-tenured, amateur, small-town politician.

Certainly the old preautomobile order in the small-town landscape was easily criticized. The grid of streets embracing the careful separation of land uses was an overly simplified idea. Railroad towns had been laid out one much like the next. Overt behavior was totally anticipated and there were few inconsistencies and few surprises from one town to another. Landscape elements were unifunctional—each building and each property had but a single purpose. Each element tended to be univalent— to have its own significance and identity unrelated to any higher unity except through proximity. The railroad town lacked subtlety.[21]

By 1960 the automobile had imposed a new order, equally as simplistic, on most towns. Orientation to the highway produced a new— not a better—order. High-speed driving was necessary for people to comprehend the logic and rhythm of the spread-out townscape, but even then the new landscape communicated disorder rather than order. The new scheme introduced fewer surprises than the old for it was even more predictable than the old. Land use and building was even more unifunctional and more univalent. The lack of planning produced a new vernacular in town building. New icons prevailed.

The Railroad's Decline

Reorientation to the automobile and the highway brought slow deterioration to, and—in many towns—eventual abandonment of, the railroad. First the passenger service, then the freight service, and finally the very physical structure of a town's railroad deteriorated. Even those towns located on the viable main lines were isolated. Joseph Lyford writes of Vandalia's two railroads: "the only concession by the Pennsylvania's 'Spirit of St. Louis' is a raucous bellow as it hurdles through a cut in the center of town an hour before noon. The I.C. is more considerate. Occasionally a freight engine shunts back and forth a few blocks outside of town to pick up some crates from one of the small factories along the tracks."[22] Many towns lost the railroad completely, the abandoned right-of-way a scar in the landscape.

Abandoned railroad at Stockton, Illinois (1972). Loss of a railroad made it more difficult for a town to market farm produce and attract new industry. With railroad abandonment, the small town turned its back completely on the railroad in favor of the highway.

Conclusion

The automobile was more than a prized possession. It promised relaxation, if only aimless wandering on the highways much as small towners had previously loitered on Main Street and around the courthouse square. The automobile promised mobility to get the small towner to other towns and nearby cities. Whether people often went to the city or not, they now realized that they could go easily and frequently. The automobile was an instrument of psychological release, for the small towner felt less trapped in his local world.

The highway intensified the small town's lack of self-respect, and its worship of the big city. As the highway was the new part of town, it symbolized progress. Yet the highway was also the service center for outsiders. It catered to a transient population, most of whom were city people full of disrespect for the small town that catered to their immediate needs. Restless youth was drawn to the highway with all of its glitter. The highway with its commercial strip was a taste of the city, albeit a poor imitation.

In most towns the highway was located more or less where the highway engineers had wanted it to go. Cost and speed of construction were usually the primary factors in such decisions. Whether the highway did or did not reinforce Main Street, or whether it destroyed a residential street or neighborhood, tended not to matter. Property owners along the highway did pretty much as they pleased in most towns. Town governments tended to encourage the highway and protect property rights along it. Most towns turned from the railroad, Main Street, and older residential neighborhoods to embrace the highway, the shopping center, and new subdivisions as symbols of progress and prosperity.

The new automobile order was implicit in a changing landscape. Changes brought to the hypothetical small town of the 1950s are diagrammed. Main Street has been widened to accommodate the major highway. Certain cross streets in the old downtown have similarly been improved. The courthouse has been relocated to the edge of town, thus speeding the flow of traffic through a much altered courthouse square. Automobile-convenient businesses with driveways and off-street parking have located around the edges of the old business district, but most new businesses are strung along the highway north of town beyond the end of Main Street, where the town's elite once lived. Houses built since 1930 are scattered around the margins of the original town grid, although the highest concentration is in the new and somewhat isolated subdivision near the country club. The town's new churches, the new high school, and the new factory are similarly located at the periphery, totally dependent upon the automobile. The railroad is partially abandoned.

As the small town came to cater to the automobile, the town as subject matter became less important to novelists and photographers alike. Few novels tied character and plot development to a town's automobile reorientation. Novelists evidently saw little of interest in the automobile's disruption of small-town life. Homer Croy's *West of the Water Tower* and Paul Horgan's *Whitewater* were exceptions. Commercial photographers continued to photograph Main Street, the courthouse, and other traditional landmarks, although the market for postcards dwindled in most

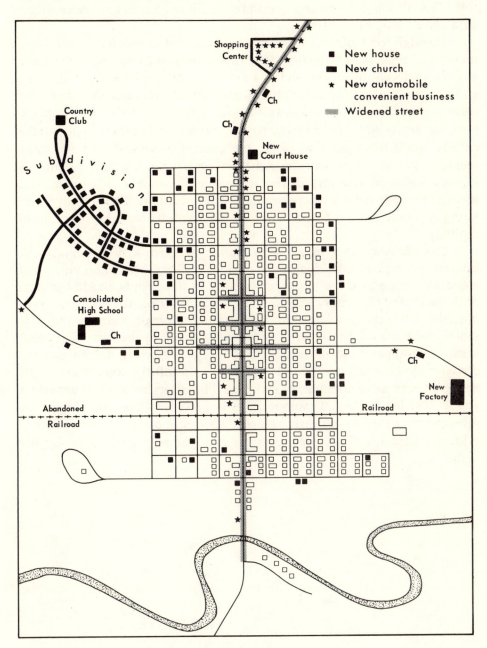

A hypothetical small town: the impact of automobile and highway.

places. Rarely did photographers venture to the highway to photograph the evolving strip. Perhaps the highway was too ephemeral, too spread out, and without enough visual distinction to attract the camera. Few novelists and few photographers saw the highway as a symbol of small-town life, although its emerging dominance in the landscape spoke otherwise for its symbolic value.

Through the 1950s the highway town was not so much an established reality as a process of transition. The future seemed to belong to the automobile, to decentralization, and to a new order of spatial organization less and less confined by the older order which would eventually be eliminated from the landscape. The highway was still a promise of things to come, a promise clearly advanced in some towns, but less so in others. Though the details varied from place to place, the general inevitability of the thing seemed assured. Some day the American small town would be entirely highway-oriented and very different as an environment. The traditional town of the railroad era was focused inward, a contained community. The highway town was focused outward through increased geographical mobility.

The highway also brought increased concern with personal self-interest, a brand of individualism less evident before. Merchants competed more and cooperated less in the remodeling of storefronts on Main Street, or in the choice of locations on the new highway strip. An "every man for himself" attitude characterized the scramble for position in the new scheme of things. The old institutions were tested in the flux of change, some to disappear and others to adjust. Less frequently did the call for community cooperation go out, and less faithfully were those calls heeded; the sense of community had been diluted, its boundaries uncertain and its core less evident. Commuters looked to the city or other towns for jobs; people shopped in outside places. The sense of community was less evident under the fluid circumstances brought and symbolized by the highway.

Eight

Small-Town Images — A Conclusion

Any inhabited landscape is a medium of communication. Its messages
may be explicit or implicit, simple or subtle.
Kevin Lynch, *Managing the Sense of a Region*

_____

At the beginning of the twentieth century most Americans lived in or
around small towns, making the small town the basic form of social
organization experienced by a majority of Americans.[1] The automobile,
among other technological and social forces, altered this situation by rein-
forcing large cities at the expense of small places. By 1960 most Americans
knew small towns only superficially as travelers on the roadside, or as images transmitted through the popular culture—images rooted more in an
idealized past than in an actual present. Novelists and photographers,
among other purveyors of popular culture, were slow to picture the social
and spatial reorientations wrought. Social scientists, with their general
neglect of small towns, have not effectively updated America's view of her
small towns. Old, outdated stereotypes persist.

Today's Stereotypes

Most Americans still feel themselves rooted somehow in a "Main
Street" America of an idealized past, where elm trees arched over streets
lined with comfortable houses—landscapes cleanly punctuated with businesses, churches, schools, and other landmarks. Paradoxically, many
Americans also feel that small towns have been parochial places, dull and
lacking in opportunities. Compared to big cities, where most Americans
have come to live, the typical small town seems changeless—neither pros-
pering nor completely failing, but just holding on as a necessary ingredient
in American geography. Both the "myth of the small town" and the
"revolt from the village," as stereotypes, are very much alive. Both views
are derived through comparison with city norms and expectations,
especially the norms and expectations of the metropolis as today's dominant place type.

Today we are told that small towns are reviving as more and more

167

Americans react negatively to big-city problems. Of course, small-town people have long held negative views of the city. In their study of "Springdale," New York, in the 1950s, Arthur Vidich and Joseph Bensman described the town's attitudes toward metropolitan life. Cities were thought to breed corruption in government, and to be too big and impersonal to be governed democratically. City social environments were seen as unwholesome, and as having an unhealthy effect on family morals. Above all, "Springdalers" thought that most of their troubles originated in cities. Their town was thought to be the victim of big-city influences.[2]

During the 1960s even urbanites came to view the nation's cities in negative terms. By the 1970s numerous surveys had disclosed a shift of residential preference from "large scale" to "small scale" places.[3] One survey revealed that two-thirds of all big-city respondents preferred to live elsewhere.[4] Only 12 percent of those who lived in small towns or in rural areas expressed preferences for other kinds of places. Another survey disclosed those qualities of place which recommended one kind of residential environment over another.[5] Small towns were seen to have the lowest taxes, the least crime, the least racial discrimination, the lowest costs of living, and the friendliest people. On the other hand, small towns were also thought to have meagre resources for shopping, recreation, education, and health care when compared to cities and suburbs. Nonetheless, the majority of respondents said they would trade metropolitan problems for affordable and safe living environments in small places.

In the early 1970s demographers detected the first signs of population shift away from the metropolises. Since there was no official census definition of the small town and thus inadequate published data, it was easier to study population shifts from metropolitan to nonmetropolitan regions. The latter areas contained no cities with populations greater than fifty thousand, and were comprised primarily of open country, villages, and towns. In the 1950s the net movement from nonmetropolitan to metropolitan areas was 5.5 million people and in the 1960s it was 2.2 million. But between 1970 and 1972 the net movement was reversed by upwards of five hundred thousand people.[6] The total number of people employed in the nonmetropolitan counties of the United States rose faster than employment in metropolitan counties. Thus the 1970s seemed to mark a historic turning point in relations between small towns and big cities.

Self-interest Versus Community: The Small-Town View

The automobile and the changes in geographical and social mobility associated with the automobile stand as the most important facets of twentieth century small-town life. The "myth of the small town" seems inseparably tied to preautomobile circumstances, where small populations focused inwardly within small spaces. It was the railroad town with its intense sense of community which sustained the myth. The automobile and the highway loosened the bonds of self-containment and more substantially pointed small towners outward in the direction of the big city. The outward flight was one of individuals seeking opportunities elsewhere.

The "myth of the small town," as a bundle of positive stereotypes favoring small-town life, reinforced the quest for traditional community; whereas the "revolt from the small town," as a bundle of negative stereotypes, encouraged individual self-interest. Never has the sense of community or individualism ever been served completely although, as value systems in American society, they have tugged and pulled at one another as if the one or the other should be allowed to triumph. Small-town landscapes of the twentieth century were symbolic of that struggle.

Main Street and the courthouse square symbolized community. The courthouse itself represented a community of government under law, but the square and Main Street were also informal meeting places—places of spontaneous neighboring so vital to community feeling. The railroad depot was another important community icon as an interface with outside places, a symbolic boundary where people entered or left their town.

The family home was a symbol of small-town individualism. Here the aspirations of men and women found ultimate expression. Through architecture and landscaping (or the lack thereof) people symbolized personal life-styles. But neighboring in the small town exerted a leveling influence on domestic display and invited conformity to middle-class norms. Minority people aside, the grid of streets with its regularity of lot size introduced a semblance of equality. The individual located himself and his family within the community as an idealized equal among equals. People sought visible display of self and family within an essentially egalitarian spatial structure where houses mixed together in a regular order, block on block. Only the relatively few gentry houses were seen to depart substantially from this pattern.

The automobile brought increased mobility, and heightened the individual's opportunities outside the family and the town. House and home were rendered less important as social reference points. The town itself was no longer as restrictive nor as important to individual identity. Automobile ownership became an imperative, and the automobile hastened conversion to a money economy dominated by large cities. Moving or commuting to large cities, and dependence upon mass media controlled from cities were symptoms of a new automobile age.

Merchants formed the small town's economic base and comprised its civic leadership. Towns were primarily mercantile places where commodities of farm and mine were assembled, and where local populations were supplied. The automobile disrupted traditional town and country ties. Merchants survived or failed on their ability to adjust to the new conditions. The sanctity of private property was asserted. Business spread out along principal thoroughfares and established itself along peripheral highways to intercept the farm and highway trade. The merchants who stayed on Main Street asserted themselves through garish advertising signs and store renovations calculated to call maximum attention to their modernity. Main Street was no longer the symbol of community so much as the symbol of frustrated individualism struggling for survival in an automobile age.

Business strung along the highway epitomized the quest for individual fulfillment under terms more flattering to the new ethic of self-assertion. Centralization was replaced by decentralization. Symbols of concentration and mutual reinforcement were replaced by symbols of separation and alienation. The new icons of place reflected a fragmented sense of purpose, and the associated beliefs and attitudes were equally as diffused. The messages transmitted by the new reality were ambiguous so far as community of interest was concerned.

The dominance of self-interest over the sense of community was reflected in the landscape in other ways. In some towns courthouses were torn down and relocated on the highway, as if to minimize the centrality of community law and order. In most towns street grids were no longer extended to absorb new house construction; detached subdivisions outside of town had come to symbolize a new freedom from traditional social restraint. New houses were isolated on large lots; neighboring was less intensive. The front porch disappeared from new houses, and fell into disuse on old.

Growth and Change: The City View

The automobile brought to small towners a new orientation to landscape. Automobiles symbolized change. The landscape, as the container of small-town life, was expected to change. Change was part of the new metropolitan universal order. The emphasis on individualism meant that there was little the community could or should do to direct change. Paradoxically, there was nothing the individual could do about change except mind his own business, and tend his own property.

Big-city people, on the other hand, have been quick to see changeless qualities in small towns. These conceptions derive, in part, from the manner by which small-town images have been communicated. Visual impressions of small towns are usually static—following closely the dictates of still photography, a principal purveyor of small-town iconography. Nor have novels fostered understanding of small towns as dynamic places.[7] Sinclair Lewis's *Main Street*, the most widely read and thus most influential of all small-town novels, is fixed in a kind of timelessness. "Gopher

Prairie" is pictured as changeless across the several years of Carol Kennicott's story. Novelists not only treated towns as static in time, but often they treated them as static in past time. Rose Wilder Lane writes of her work of the 1930s:

> Today the small town point of view is not only in the small towns; and the city's point of view, formed by experience with machines and viewing masses of men as mechanisms, is to be met far from cities. When I found the American small town interesting to me as material for fiction, I had to return to the small town of about thirty years ago.[8]

Social scientists have also prompted a static small-town view. Art Gallaher's *Plainville Fifteen Years Later* stands as a significant exception.[9] Demographers have shown interest in small-town change, but are much hindered by the lack of adequate census definition regarding small towns as a distinctive place type—thus they lack appropriate data for analysis. Of course, the whole of social science has been and continues to be biased toward study of America's metropolises, the most dynamic and expansive of social settings.

Most American towns are small because they simply did not grow. Few towns ever deliberately decided not to grow; growth, or the lack thereof, was usually dictated by circumstances beyond a town's control. In an urban-oriented society which has valued bigness, growth has dominated the idea of success. This was true even where people were forced by circumstances at least to consider the positive aspects of smallness. The claim by many small towners that they do not wish to live in big places may be, in part, a sincere belief in the small scale of doing things, resulting from years of seeking the positive in small-town circumstances. But it is also a rationalization of the all too obvious situation of no growth or slow growth. The fact remains that the successful small towns of the past are no longer small. They are cities. To most city people, small towns, because of their smallness, are stereotypes of the unsuccessful.

Change is, of course, a relative matter for where change is not dramatic it is easily overlooked. Where an important landmark, like the courthouse, survives or where the integrity of a key area, like Main Street, has remained relatively undisturbed, people may be blinded to changes elsewhere—as, for example, the drift of Main Street commerce to peripheral highway locations. The highway strip outside of the town does not impress like its big-city counterparts.

The Study of Small-Town Images

Understanding the place symbolism inherent in photographs, novels, and other forms of popular culture seems to me an important endeavor.

171

People behave not so much according to reality, as to reality conceptualized. It is the image of place that is important. If small towns are to be understood as places, understanding must embrace the systems of belief, attitude, and icon by which they have been known. But for a place image to be understood, it is also necessary to know the media by which the image has been communicated.

Postcard photographers sought the unique in small-town landscapes, but tended to find the typical instead. Every town had features which stood as icons of locality, but there was great similarity from town to town. Views of Main Street clearly symbolized a town's worth as a place. If not Main Street, then a view of the courthouse, the railroad depot, the high school, or a residential street would do. These were standard images which dominated people's conceptions of what typified small-town environments.

Snapshot photography tended to emphasize people, although where people were pictured was nearly as important as the people themselves. Photographs taken at home on the front porch or in the front yard predominated. Relatively few snapshots were taken at work, either in the home or at the shop, mill, or mine. As amateur photography was a form of relaxation, many snapshots pictured leisure time. Pictures of picnics or trips to the countryside, where lakes and wooded stream banks figured prominently, were common. Attempts to portray oneself as special led to a search for unique settings in which to be photographed. But people tended to find the same photographic contrivances interesting, thus making the search for uniqueness typical.

Novelists emphasized the typical in small-town places. Towns not only proved of manageable scale for plot and character development; but, because they were so stereotyped in the American consciousness, the novelist was able to use them as a kind of shorthand in developing a book's setting. The American reading public knew what small towns were all about, and could read into the symbolism of a novel's landscape much which the novelist left unsaid. Only regionalists, like William Faulkner or Hamilton Basso, seemed to tarry over the details of landscape which made their towns distinctive from the American mainstream.[10] Novelists like Sherwood Anderson, Rose Wilder Lane, and Sinclair Lewis were regionalists also, but their region was the Midwest. "Winesburg," the "Old Home Town," and "Gopher Prairie," were viewed by readers as the American mainstream due to their Midwestern flavor.[11] Novelists who wanted typical small towns usually chose Midwestern prototypes.

Social science sought generalization. Much like the novelist, the social scientist found the small town easy to understand for the small scale and relative simplicity of size. Places like "Plainville," "Elmtown," and "Mineville" were chosen for their typical qualities.[12] Researchers hoped to generalize from case studies to small towns at large, and beyond to American society. The literature of social science has done little to teach Americans about the unique qualities of individual places. Instead, social scientists have strengthened the view that small towns do comprise a distinctive place type in the American experience—that American small towns are, indeed, very much alike everywhere.

Reassessing Small Towns

Today's small towns should be assessed not only as places distinctive unto themselves, but as representing a distinctive place type—a distinctive kind of American environment or habitat. Assessment should include the extent to which various value systems are, and have been, symbolized in local landscape. Townscapes should be managed as resources for their symbolic as well as functional values. Unfortunately, most small towns today share a pessimistic conservatism bred of decades of stability or decline. The triumph of the "revolt" over the "myth" makes such assessment difficult. Peirce Lewis writes of Bellefonte, Pennsylvania:

> Three generations of economic trouble, three generations of watching Bellefonte children leave town upon reaching adulthood, three generations of being told incessantly that Bellefonte was a tired worthless place—all these have carried the town beyond the threshold of pain to a state of pessimism and resignation which often approaches despair. Out of pessimism has come kind of grim conservatism that has little necessarily to do with political attitudes. It reflects the fear shared by passengers in a sinking lifeboat that any movement, any change threatens survival itself.[13]

Most small towns have been torn between the desire to grow and be prosperous, and the inability to do so. As Peirce Lewis points out, small towns fear stability for there is little in the national experience to prepare a community to accept slow growth or, perhaps, no growth at all: "nothing, in short, which prepares it to grow old gracefully."[14] It has always seemed best for towns to emulate the successes of the city, hoping to be successful, too.

After World War II most small towns evolved in the image of big-city suburbs. The highway dimension of small-town life was emphasized. Change along the highway meant progress and progress spelled success, albeit limited success. Bearing few symbols of success of their own, small-town people borrowed the symbols which epitomized successful place-making elsewhere. "Suburbanized" small towns brought America closer to a homogenized national landscape, where every place and every kind of place looked very much the same—a reflection of a new metropolitan

173

universal order. Should this trend continue, small towns will have lost the opportunity to develop as distinctive places in their own right, and to use those distinctions to amplify intrinsic social advantages.

Small towns must dare to be different, and to preserve difference in the environment besides. As Robert Riley writes of rural America: "If the countryside is to prosper it must be different from city or suburb. Not better, for that is a matter of individual taste, but different."[15] Perhaps the town can offer small-scale community reflected and symbolized in a simplistic landscape of limited extent. In a small town the individual is one among relatively few. This sense of identity is easily translated into personalized place attachments where the symbols of landscape are few and thus frequently relied upon. Perhaps the small town can offer a different sense of time where the pace of life is slower, and where things, especially things in the landscape, do not change rapidly. The small town rooted in agriculture reflects the seasonality of planting and harvest, and of nature generally. Life is more cyclical as opposed to the linear, open-ended sense of activity felt in the city.

Small towns present the nation with both a challenge and an opportunity. They can demonstrate, to borrow words from Donald Connery, "that a genuine civilized life on a human scale, however imperfect, still exists and is still possible in the U.S.A."[16] Connery continues: "Such communities are precious resources, well worth preserving and fighting for. . . . I, for one, find it reassuring to have so close at hand so much evidence of individual self-reliance, self-confidence, good humor, good manners, concern for neighbors, readiness to lend a helping hand, pride in town and nation, and respect for the natural world."[17] Elva Miller, another commentator on America's small towns, concludes: "The country town is not merely the embryo of, or the foundation for, a city. It is something far different that has no cause to grow out of itself into something else."[18]

The images which characterized American small towns in the early twentieth century were varied. Some were explicit, others subtle. Community and self-interest were variously symbolized, along with other values. Main Street, the courthouse, and the depot were easily recognized as icons associated with the community-making impulse. The highway as a symbol of individualism was less overt, the ties to prevailing beliefs and attitudes about small towns less clear. Identifying and managing the traditional icons of place can provide a catalyst and focus for small-town development today. Concern with the communalities of landscape from place to place can strengthen the belief in small-town America as a distinctive kind of environment worth protecting.

NOTES

Preface

1. Donald W. Meinig, "Symbolic Landscapes: Some Idealizations of American Communities," in *The Interpretation of Ordinary Landscapes,* ed. D. W. Meinig (New York: Oxford University Press, 1979), p. 167.

Chapter One

1. Harold S. Williams, "Smallness and the Small Town," *Small Town* 18 (October 1977): 11.
2. See especially Zona Gale, *Friendship Village* (New York: MacMillan, 1908); Sarah Orne Jewett, *The Country of the Pointed Firs* (New York: Anchor, 1956); Meredith Nicholson, *A Hoosier Chronicle* (Boston: Houghton Mifflin, 1912); and Booth Tarkington, *The Gentleman from Indiana* (New York: Doubleday and McClure, 1900).
3. Carl Van Doren, "Sinclair Lewis and the Revolt from the Village," in *Twentieth Century Interpretations of Arrowsmith: A Collection of Critical Essays,* ed. Robert J. Griffen (Englewood Cliffs, N.J.: Prentice-Hall, 1968), p. 83.
4. Zona Gale, *Friendship Village Love Stories* (New York: MacMillan, 1909), p. 6.
5. Ibid.
6. Lewis Atherton, "The Midwestern Country Town—Myth and Reality," *Agricultural History* 26 (July 1952): 73.
7. Page Smith, *As a City Upon a Hill: The Town in American History* (New York: Knopf, 1966), p. 209.
8. Ibid.
9. See especially Theodore Dreiser, *Sister Carrie* (New York: Doubleday, Page, 1900); Sherwood Anderson, *Winesburg, Ohio* (New York: Random House, 1910); Edgar Lee Masters, *Spoon River Anthology* (New York: Crowell, 1916); and Sinclair Lewis, *Main Street* (New York: New American Library, 1961).
10. Van Doren, "Sinclair Lewis," p. 83. See also Anthony C. Hilfer, *The Revolt from the Village, 1915–1930* (Chapel Hill, N.C.: University of North Carolina Press, 1969), p. 30.
11. Wallace Stegner, *Second Growth* (Boston: Houghton Mifflin, 1947), p. 61.
12. Van Doren, "Sinclair Lewis," p. 86.
13. Sinclair Lewis, *Main Street,* p. 37.
14. Ibid., p. 154.
15. D. J. Dooley, *The Art of Sinclair Lewis* (Lincoln: University of Nebraska Press, 1967), p. 61.
16. Richard O'Connor, *Sinclair Lewis* (New York: McGraw-Hill, 1971), p. 10.
17. Kenneth E. Boulding, *The Image* (Ann Arbor: University of Michigan Press, 1956); and Daniel J. Boorstin, *The Image: A Guide to Pseudo-Events in America* (New York: Harper, 1964).
18. For an introduction to the literature of environmental cognition and the concept of the behavioral environment, see Gary T. Moore and Reginald G. Golledge, eds., *En-

175

vironmental Knowing (Stroudsburg, Pa.: Dowden, Hutchinson, and Ross, 1976); and J. Douglas Porteous, *Environment and Behavior* (Reading, Mass.: Addison-Wesley, 1977).

19. See Roger C. Barker, *Ecological Psychology* (Stanford: Stanford University Press, 1968).
20. Smith, *As a City*, p. 259.
21. Ibid., p. 258.
22. Stegner, *Second Growth*, p. ii.
23. Theodore Dreiser, *A Hoosier Holiday* (New York: John Lane, 1916), p. 448.
24. Noel Houston, *The Great Promise* (New York: Reynal and Hitchcock, 1946), p. 213.
25. For an introduction to the literature, see Roland L. Warren, *The Community in America* (Chicago: Rand McNally, 1963); and Maurice R. Stein, *The Eclipse of Community: An Interpretation of American Studies* (Princeton: Princeton University Press, 1960).
26. Albert Blumenthal, *Small Town Stuff* (Chicago: University of Chicago Press, 1932), p. 39.
27. Ibid., p. 110.

Chapter Two

1. Houston, *Great Promise*, pp. 87, 118, and 195.
2. Ibid., p. 198.
3. Tarkington, *Gentleman*, p. 1.
4. Sinclair Lewis, *Main Street*, p. 229.
5. Ibid., p. 6.
6. Carole Rifkind, *Main Street: The Face of Urban America* (New York: Harper, 1977), p. 63.
7. W. L. White, *What People Said* (New York: Viking, 1938), p. 77.
8. Madison Cooper, *Sironia, Texas* (Boston: Houghton Mifflin, 1952), p. 38.
9. Lewis Atherton, *Main Street on the Middle Border* (Bloomington: Indiana University Press, 1954), p. 57.
10. Ferdinand Reyher, *I Heard Them Sing* (Boston: Little, Brown, 1946), p. 81.
11. Homer Croy, *West of the Water Tower* (New York: Grosset and Dunlap, 1923), p. 25.
12. David Lavender, "A Rocky Mountain Fantasy: Telluride, Colorado," in *A Vanishing America: The Life and Times of the Small Town*, ed. Thomas C. Wheeler (New York: Holt, Rinehart, and Winston, 1964), p. 143.
13. See William Faulkner, *The Town* (New York: Vintage, 1961).
14. Atherton, *Main Street*, p. 148.
15. Larry Woiwode, *Beyond the Bedroom Wall: A Family Album* (New York: Avon, 1976), p. 9.
16. Rose Wilder Lane, *Old Home Town* (New York: Longmans, Green, 1935), p. 10.
17. Atherton, *Main Street*, p. 117.
18. Ibid., p. 128.
19. See Edward T. Price, Jr., "The Central Courthouse Square in the American County Seat," *Geographical Review* 58 (1968): 29–60.
20. Lane, *Old Home Town*, p. i.
21. William Faulkner, *Requiem for a Nun* (New York: Random House, 1951), p. 40.
22. Ibid., p. 28.
23. Price, "Central Courthouse Square," p. 59.
24. Tarkington, *Gentleman*, p. 2.
25. Ross Lockridge, *Raintree County* (Boston: Houghton Mifflin, 1947), p. 380.
26. Ibid.
27. Atherton, *Main Street*, p. 38.
28. Ibid.
29. Tarkington, *Gentleman*, p. 3.

30. See George Hilton and John F. Due, *The Electric Interurban Railways in America* (Palo Alto: Stanford University Press, 1960).
31. Sinclair Lewis, *Main Street*, p. 27.
32. Mary King, *Quince Bolliver* (Boston: Houghton Mifflin, 1941), p. 48.
33. Ibid., p. 25.
34. Sinclair Lewis, *Main Street,* p. 114.
35. Newell L. Sims, *A Hoosier Village*, Studies in History, Economics, and Public Law, no. 117 (New York: Columbia University, 1912), p. 41.
36. Ibid., p. 81.
37. Ibid., p. 35.
38. Robert Penn Warren, *The Circus in the Attic: And Other Stories* (New York: Harcourt, Brace, 1931), p. 3.
39. Jack Conroy, "Boyhood in a Coal Town," *The American Mercury* 23 (May 1931): 83.
40. Philip D. Strong, *The Iron Mountain* (New York: Farrar and Rinehart, 1942), p. 17.

Chapter Three

1. Rifkind, *Main Street*, p. 17.
2. Houston, *Great Promise*, p. 173.
3. See Paul C. Morrison, "A Morphological Study of Worthington, Ohio," *Ohio Journal of Science* (January 1934): 38.
4. M. R. Wolfe, "Small Town, Puget Sound Region," *Landscape* 9 (winter 1959–60): 11.
5. Booth Tarkington, *The Conquest of Canaan* (New York: Harper, 1905), p. 28.
6. J. B. Jackson, *American Space* (New York: Norton, 1972), p. 37.
7. Croy, *West of the Water Tower*, p. 65.
8. Tarkington, *Conquest*, p. 29.
9. Houston, *Great Promise,* p. 250.
10. W. L. White, *What People Said*, p. 4.
11. May T. Watts, *Reading the Landscape* (New York: Collier, 1975), p. 320.
12. Atherton, *Main Street*, p. 23.
13. James West, *Plainville U.S.A.* (New York: Columbia University Press, 1946), p. 119.
14. Ibid., p. 115.
15. Ibid., p. 116.
16. Atherton, *Main Street*, p. 105.
17. Sinclair Lewis, *Main Street*, p. 241.
18. Lane, *Old Home Town*, p. 6.
19. Ibid., p. 8.
20. R. L. Duffus, *Williamstown Branch: Impersonal Memoirs of a Vermont Boyhood* (New York: Norton, 1958), p. 26.
21. James West, *Plainville*, p. 36.
22. Art Gallaher, Jr., *Plainville Fifteen Years Later* (New York: Columbia University Press, 1961), p. 96.
23. James West, *Plainville*, p. 36.
24. Ibid.
25. Ibid., p. 35.
26. Sinclair Lewis, *Main Street*, p. 392.
27. Harlan P. Douglass, *The Little Town* (New York: Macmillan, 1919), p. 18.
28. Ibid., p. 19.
29. Lane, *Old Home Town,* p. 6.
30. [J. B. Jackson], "Notes and Comments," *Landscape* 17 (autumn 1967): 2.
31. Strong, *Iron Mountain,* p. 20.
32. August B. Hollingshead, *Elmstown's Youth: The Impact of Social Classes on Adolescents* (New York: Wiley, 1949), p. 62.

33. Hamilton Basso, *Court House Square* (New York: Scribner's, 1936), p. 247.
34. Sherwood Anderson, *Hello Towns!* (New York: Liveright, 1929), p. 82.
35. R. L. Duffus, *The Waterbury Record* (New York: Norton, 1959), p. 243.
36. Pamela West, "The Rise and Fall of the American Porch," *Landscape* 20 (spring 1976): 45.
37. James West, *Plainville,* p. 100.
38. Ibid.
39. Ibid. p., 102.
40. Ibid., p. 103.
41. Blumenthal, *Small Town Stuff,* p. 136
42. Ibid., p. 124.
43. James West, *Plainville,* p. 70.
44. Willa Cather, *My Antonia* (Boston: Houghton Mifflin, 1918), p. 228.
45. Hilfer, *Revolt from the Village,* p. 87
46. Cather, *My Antonia,* p. 249.
47. Hilfer, *Revolt from the Village,* p. 162.
48. Ibid., p. 163.
49. Sims, *Hoosier Village,* p. 166.
50. Blumenthal, *Small Town Stuff,* p. 399.
51. Arthur J. Vidich and Joseph Bensman, *Small Town in Mass Society: Class, Power, and Religion in a Rural Community* (Garden City, N.Y.: Anchor, 1969), p. 74.
52. James West, *Plainville,* p. 14.
53. Atherton, *Main Street,* p. 106.
54. Vidich and Bensman, *Small Town,* p. 32.

Chapter Four

1. Thornton Wilder, *Our Town: A Play in Three Acts* (New York: Coward McCann, 1938), p. 58.
2. Gale, *Friendship Village Love Stories,* p. 26.
3. Sinclair Lewis, *Main Street.*
4. H. L. Mencken, "Americana," *The American Mercury,* 8 (June 1926): 169.
5. [The Country Contributor] "The Ideas of a Plain Country Woman," *The Ladies Home Journal* 31 (March 1914): 36.
6. Lane, *Old Home Town,* p. 11.
7. Reyher, *I Heard Them,* p. 90.
8. Blumenthal, *Small Town Stuff,* p. 136.
9. Zona Gale, *Birth* (New York: Macmillian, 1923), p. 71.
10. Blumenthal, *Small Town Stuff,* p. 95.
11. Gale, *Birth,* p. 70.
12. Gallaher, *Plainville,* p. 15.
13. Gale, *Birth,* p. 72.
14. Blumenthal, *Small Town Stuff,* p. 96.
15. Gale, *Birth,* p. 72.
16. Ibid., p. 73.
17. Blumenthal, *Small Town Stuff,* p. 96.
18. Sinclair Lewis, *Main Street,* p. 66.
19. Basso, *Court House Square,* p. 69.
20. Lane, *Old Home Town,* p. 19.
21. Vidich and Bensman, *Small Town,* p. 4.
22. Lane, *Old Home Town,* p. 19.
23. Ibid., p. 15.
24. Sherwood Anderson, *Home Town* (New York: Alliance, 1940), p. 30.
25. [The Country Contributor] "The Ideas of a Plain Country Woman," *The Ladies Home Journal* 30 (August 1913): p. 26.
26. Sherwood Anderson, *Home Town,* p. 41.

27. Ibid., p. 52.
28. Ibid., p. 87.
29. Ibid., p. 20.
30. Atherton, *Main Street,* p. 200.
31. Bruce Catton, *Waiting for the Morning Train, An American Boyhood* (Garden City, N.Y.: Doubleday, 1972), p. 39.
32. Basso, *Court House Square,* p. 207.
33. Dorothy James Roberts, *A Man of Malice Landing* (New York: Macmillian, 1943), p. 105.
34. Smith, *As a City,* p. 215.
35. Ibid., p. 216.
36. William Allen White, *The Autobiography of William Allen White* (New York: Macmillan, 1946), p. 67.
37. Quoted in O'Connor, *Sinclair Lewis,* p. 14.
38. James West, *Plainville,* p. 163.
39. Ibid., p. 110.
40. Dreiser, *Hoosier Holiday,* p. 278.
41. Elizabeth M. Kerr, *Yoknapatawpha; Faulkner's "Little Postage Stamp of Native Soil"* (New York: Fordham University Press, 1969), p. 118.
42. Dreiser, *Hoosier Holiday,* p. 434.
43. Smith, *As a City,* p. 219.
44. Bishop John H. Vincent, quoted in Gregory Mason, "Chatauqua: Its Technic," *The American Mercury* 1 (February 1924): 275.
45. Mason, "Chatauqua," p. 279.
46. Dreiser, *Hoosier Holiday,* p. 341.

Chapter Five

1. Thorstein Veblen, "The Country Town," *The Freeman* 11 (July 1923): 418.
2. Sherwood Anderson, *Hello Towns!,* p. 66.
3. Sims, *Hoosier Village,* p. 57.
4. Smith, *As a City,* p. 200.
5. Douglass, *Little Town,* p. 83.
6. Veblen, "Country Town," p. 442.
7. Faulkner, *The Town.*
8. Croy, *West of the Water Tower,* p. 64.
9. Woiwode, *Beyond the Bedroom Wall,* p. 9.
10. Dreiser, *Hoosier Holiday,* p. 480.
11. Sims, *Hoosier Village,* p. 64
12. Ibid., p. 97.
13. Edmund De S. Brunner, *Village Communities* (Garden City, N.Y.: Doubleday, Doran, 1938), p. 71.
14. Charles Givens, *All Cats Are Gray* (Indianapolis: Bobbs-Merrill, 1937), p. 109.
15. Tarkington, *Conquest,* p. 28.
16. Duffus, *Waterbury Record,* p. 84.
17. Stephen W. Sears, Murray Belsky, and Douglas Tunstell, *Hometown U.S.A.* (New York: American Heritage, 1975), p. 78.
18. Duffus, *Waterbury Record,* p. 127.
19. See George S. Bobinski, *Carnegie Libraries: Their History and Impact on American Public Library Development* (Chicago: American Library Association, 1969); and Durand R. Miller, *Carnegie Grants for Library Buildings, 1890–1917* (New York: The Carnegie Corporation, 1943).
20. See Vidich and Bensman, *Small Town.*
21. James West, *Plainville,* p. 80.
22. Lane, *Old Home Town,* p. 3.
23. Smith, *As a City,* p. 25.

24. R. H. Knapp and H. B. Goodrich, *Origins of American Scientists* (Chicago: University of Chicago Press, 1952), p. 291.
25. Harold Sinclair, *Years of Illusion* (New York: Doubleday, Doran, 1941), p. 11.
26. Ibid., p. 9.

Chapter Six

1. Catton, *Waiting,* p. 38.
2. Sims, *Hoosier Village,* p. 118
3. James West, *Plainville,* p. 17.
4. Gallaher, *Plainville,* p. 23.
5. Ibid., p. 24.
6. James West, *Plainville,* p. 211.
7. Lane, *Old Home Town,* p. 2.
8. James West, *Plainville,* p. 40.
9. W. L. White, *What People Said,* p. 77.
10. James West, *Plainville,* p. 59.
11. Reyher, *I Heard Them,* p. 123.
12. Ibid., p. 185.
13. Atherton, *Main Street,* p. 237.
14. For an excellent case study, see Norman T. Moline, *Mobility and the Small Town, 1900–1930,* Department of Geography, Research Paper no. 132, (Chicago: University of Chicago, 1971).
15. A. H. Anderson, *The Expanding Rural Community* ([Lincoln] University of Nebraska Agriculture Experiment Station, 1961), p. 5.
16. [H. L. Mencken], "Are Small Towns Doomed?", *The American Mercury* 32 (May 1934): 75.
17. W. L. White, *What People Said,* p. 271.
18. James West, *Plainville,* p. 22.
19. Gallaher, *Plainville*, p. 16.
20. [Mencken], "Are Small Towns Doomed?", p. 75.
21. Blumenthal, *Small Town Stuff,* p. 55.
22. Gallaher, *Plainville,* p. 84.
23. Ibid.
24. Atherton, *Main Street,* p. 240.
25. James West, *Plainville,* p. 18.
26. Sinclair Lewis, *Main Street,* p. 133.
27. Elva A. Miller, *Town and Country* (Chapel Hill: University of North Carolina Press, 1928), p. 13.
28. Arnold Paulsen and Jerry Carlson, "Is Rural Main Street Disappearing?", *Better Farming Methods* 33 (December 1961), p. 13.
29. Joseph P. Lyford, *The Talk of Vandalia* (New York: Harper, 1964), pp. 9, 10.
30. W. L. White, *What People Said,* p. 8.
31. Gallaher, *Plainville,* p. 233.
32. Peirce Lewis, "Small Town in Pennsylvania," *Annals, Association of American Geographers* 62 (June 1972): 326.
33. Rifkind, *Main Street,* p. 222.
34. J. B. Jackson, "The Almost Perfect Town,"*Landscape* 2 (spring 1952): 3.
35. Ibid., p. 4.
36. Croy, *West of the Water Tower,* p. 25.
37. Dreiser, *Hoosier Holiday,* p. 135.
38. Peirce Lewis, "Small Town," p. 347.
39. King, *Quince Bolliver,* p. 22.
40. W. L. White, *What People Said,* p. 118.
41. Givens, *All Cats,* p. 24.
42. Edmund De S. Brunner, Gwendolyn S. Hughes, and Marjorie Patten, *American

    Agricultural Villages (New York: Doron, 1927), p. 224.
43. Woiwode, *Beyond the Bedroom Wall,* p. 9.
44. Basso, *Court House Square,* p. 64.
45. W. L. White, *What People Said,* p. 5.
46. Gallaher, *Plainville,* p. 78.
47. W. L. White, *What People Said,* p. 5.
48. Dreiser, *Hoosier Holiday,* p. 288.
49. Paul Corey, *County Seat* (Indianapolis: Bobbs-Merrill, 1941), p. 107.
50. Atherton, *Main Street,* p. 43.
51. James West, *Plainville,* p. 10.
52. Atherton, *Main Street,* p. 61.
53. Lyford, *Talk of Vandalia,* pp. 45, 46.
54. Smith, *As a City,* p. 104.
55. Mary E. Wilkins, *The Portion of Labor* (New York: Harper, 1901), p. 16.
56. Faulkner, *The Town.*
57. Kerr, *Yoknapatawpha,* p. 49.
58. James West, *Plainville,* p. 13.
59. Gallaher, *Plainville,* p. 94.
60. James West, *Plainville,* p. 16.
61. Gallaher, *Plainville,* p. 26.

Chapter Seven

1. Atherton, *Main Street,* p. 237.
2. Croy, *West of the Water Tower,* p. 358.
3. Donald S. Connery, *One American Town* (New York: Simon and Schuster, 1972), p. 38.
4. Peirce Lewis, "Small Town," p. 347.
5. Sherwood Anderson, *Home Town,* pp. 33, 40.
6. Gallaher, *Plainville,* p. 22.
7. [Jackson], "Notes and Comments," p. 1.
8. Robert Riley, "New Mexico Villages in a Future Landscape," *Landscape* 18 (winter 1969): 8.
9. J. B. Jackson, "Metamorphosis," *Annals, Association of American Geographers* 62 (June 1972): 156.
10. Sherwood Anderson, *Home Town,* p. 40.
11. See John Baeder, *Diners* (New York: Abrams, 1978).
12. Dreiser, *Hoosier Holiday,* p. 120.
13. Jackson, "The Almost Perfect Town," p. 8.
14. George R. Stewart, *U.S. 40: Cross Section of the United States* (Boston: Houghton Mifflin, 1953), p. 246.
15. Ibid., p. 247.
16. Jack Kerouac, *On the Road* (New York: Viking, 1955).
17. Lyford, *Talk of Vandalia,* p. 71.
18. Ibid.
19. Paul Horgan, *Whitewater* (New York: Farrar, Straus, and Giroux, 1969), p. 75.
20. A. W. Fawcett, Jr., "Help for the Village," *Landscape* 7 (autumn 1957): 8.
21. See E. Relph, *Place and Placelessness* (London: Pion, 1976), p. 136.
22. Lyford, *Talk of Vandalia,* p. 3.

Chapter Eight

1. Smith, *As a City,* p. vii.
2. Vidich and Bensman, *Small Town,* p. 33.
3. See Duane Elgin et al., *City Size and the Quality of Life: An Analysis of the Policy Implications of Continued Population Concentration* (Washington, D.C.: U.S.

Government Printing Office, 1974), p. A-3. For the opinion surveys reported, see Roper Opinion Poll, October 1948, in E. S. Lee et al., *An Introduction to Urban Decentralization Research* (Springdale, Va.: National Technical Information Source, U.S. Department of Commerce, 1971); and the Gallup Opinion Survey, March 1966 and February 1970, in "Public Attitudes Towards Population Distribution Issues," in *Population Distribution and Policy, Part 5* (Washington, D.C.: U.S. Government Printing Office, 1972).

4. Elgin et al., *City Size*, p. 29.
5. "Americans View their Communities," Chicago *Tribune,* 16 April 1978, p. 6.
6. David W. Hacker, "Back to the Boonies: Small Towns Thrive as Urban Migration Reverses," *The National Observer,* 5 January 1974, p. 1.
7. James Michener's *Centennial* (New York: Random House, 1974) is an exception, although it is intended more as a regional history than a town history.
8. Lane, *Old Home Town*, p. 25.
9. Gallaher, *Plainville.*
10. See Calvin S. Brown, "Faulkner's Geography and Topography," *Publications of the Modern Language Association of America* 77 (1962): 652–59.
11. Atherton, "Midwestern Country Town," p. 73.
12. James West, *Plainville*; Gallaher, *Plainville*; Hollingshead, *Elmtown's Youth*; Blumenthal, *Small Town Stuff.*
13. Peirce Lewis, "Small Town," p. 349.
14. Ibid., p. 323.
15. Riley, "New Mexico Villages," p. 5.
16. Connery, *One American Town,* p. 15.
17. Ibid., p. 16.
18. Miller, *Town and Country*, p. 141.

BIBLIOGRAPHY

Aldrich, Bess Streeter. "Why I Live in a Small Town." *The Ladies Home Journal* 50 (June 1933): 21 and 61.

Allen, Irving L. "Community Size, Population Composition, and Cultural Activity in Smaller Communities." *Rural Sociology,* 33 (September 1968): 328–38.

"Americana." *The American Mercury* 8 (June 1926): 169.

"Americans View Their Communities." Chicago *Tribune,* 16 April 1978, p. 6.

Anderson, A. H. *The Expanding Rural Community.* [Lincoln] University of Nebraska Agricultural Experiment Station, 1961.

——— and Miller, C. J. *The Changing Role of the Small Town in Farm Areas.* Bulletin 419. Lincoln: Nebraska Agricultural Experiment Station, 1953).

Anderson, Sherwood. *Hello Towns!* New York: Liveright, 1929.

———*Home Town.* New York: Alliance, 1940.

———*Winesburg Ohio.* New York: Random House, 1910.

Anderson, Wilbert L. *The Country Town.* New York: Baker and Taylor, 1906.

Atherton, Lewis. *Main Street on the Middle Border.* Bloomington: Indiana University Press, 1954.

———"The Midwestern Country Town: Myth and Reality." *Agricultural History,* 26 (July 1952): 73–80.

Baeder, John. *Diners.* New York: Abrams, 1978.

Barker, Roger G., and Wright, Herbert F. *Midwest and Its Children: The Psychological Ecology of an American Town.* 1955. Reprint. Hamden, Conn.: Archon, 1971.

Basso, Hamilton. *Court House Square.* New York: Scribner's, 1936.

Bastian, Robert. "Store-Front Remodeling in Small Midwestern Cities, 1890–1940." *Pioneer America Society Transactions* 1 (1978): 1–14.

Bauder, Ward W. *The Impact of Population on Rural Community Life: The Economic System.* Ames: Iowa State University Press, 1962.

Baumann, Ruth. *The Town in Wisconsin.* Extension Service Circular 599. Madison: University of Wisconsin, 1961.

Berger, Michael L. *The Devil Wagon in God's Country: The Automobile and Social Change in Rural America, 1893–1929.* Hamden, Conn.: Archon, 1979.

Blumenthal, Albert. *A Sociological Study of a Small Town.* Chicago: University of Chicago Press, 1932.

———. *Small Town Stuff.* Chicago: University of Chicago Press, 1932.

Boorstin, Daniel J. *The Image: A Guide to Pseudo-Events in America.* New York: Harper, 1964.

Boulding, Kenneth E. *The Image.* Ann Arbor: University of Michigan Press, 1956.

Brown, Calvin S. "Faulkner's Geography and Topography." *Publications of the Modern Language Association* 77 (December 1962): 652–59.

Brunner, Edmund De S. *Village Communities.* Garden City, N.Y.: Doubleday, Doran, 1928.

———; Hughes, Gwendolyn S.; and Patten, Marjorie. *American Agricultural Villages.* New York: Doran, 1927.

Buckley, G. T. "Is Oxford the Original of Jefferson in William Faulkner's Novels?" *Publications of the Modern Language Association* 76 (September 1961): 447–54.

Cather, Willa. *My Antonia.* Boston: Houghton Mifflin, 1918.

Catherwood, Mary H. *The Spirit of an Illinois Town.* Boston: Houghton Mifflin, 1897.

Catton, Bruce. *Waiting for the Morning Train: An American Boyhood.* Garden City, N.Y.: Doubleday, 1972.

Chase, Edwin T. "Forty Years on Main Street." *Iowa Journal of History and Politics* 34 (July 1936): 227–61

Commission on Population Growth and the American Future. *Population Distribution and Policy.* Washington, D.C.: U.S. Government Printing Office, 1972.

Connery, Donald S. *One American Town.* New York: Simon and Schuster, 1977.

Conroy, Jack. "Boyhood in a Coal Town." *The Amercian Mercury* 23 (May 1931): 83–92.

Cooper, Madison A. *Sironia, Texas.* Boston: Houghton Mifflin, 1952.

Corey, Paul. *County Seat.* Indianapolis: Bobbs-Merrill, 1941.

[The Country Contributor] "The Ideas of a Plain Country Woman." *The Ladies Home Journal* 30 (August 1913): 26 and 31 (March 1914): 36.

Croy, Homer. *West of the Water Tower.* New York: Harper, 1923.

Doerr, Arthur H., and Morris, John W. "Oklahoma Panhandle." *Landscape* 10 (fall 1960): 32–35.

Dooley, D. J. *The Art of Sinclair Lewis.* Lincoln: University of Nebraska Press, 1967.

Douglas, Harlan P. *The Little Town.* New York: Macmillan, 1919.

Dreiser, Theodore. *A Hoosier Holiday.* New York: John Lane, 1916.

———. *Sister Carrie.* New York: Doubleday, Page, 1900.

Driscoll, Charles B. "Amercian Portraits VII. The Country Banker." *The American Mercury* 3 (September 1924): 88–92.

Duffus, R. L. *The Waterbury Record.* New York: Norton, 1959.

———. *Williamstown Branch: Impersonal Memoirs of a Vermont Boyhood.* New York: Norton, 1958.

Dunbar, Willis F. "The Opera House as a Social Institution in Michigan." *Michigan History Magazine* 27 (October–December 1943): 661–72.

Edwards, A. D. *Beaverdam: A Rural Community in Transition.* Bulletin 340. Blacksburg, Va.: Agricultural Experiment Station, 1942.

Elgin, Duane; Thomas, Tom; Logothetti, Tom; and Cox, Sue. *City Size and the Quality of Life: An Analysis of the Policy Implications of Continued Population Concentration.* Washington, D.C.: U.S. Government Printing Office, 1974.

Faulkner, William. *Requiem for a Nun.* New York: Random House, 1951.

———. *The Town.* New York: Vintage, 1961.

Fawcett, A. W., Jr. "Help for the Village." *Landscape* 7 (autumn 1957): 6–10.

Folse, C. L. "Growth and Decline of Illinois Villages 1950 to 1960." *Journal of Agricultural Economics* 6 (January 1966): 11–16.

Francaviglia, Richard. "Main Street Revisited." *Places* 1 (October 1974): 7–11.

———. "The View from Main Street." *Antipode* 7 (December 1975): 46–50.

Fry, Luther. *American Villagers.* New York: Doran, 1926.

Fuguitt, Glenn V. "County Seat Status as a Factor in Small Town Growth and Decline." *Social Forces* 44 (December 1965): 245–51.

———. "The Places Left Behind: Population Trends and Policy for Rural America." *Rural Sociology* 36 (December 1971): 449–70.

——— and Thomas, Donald W. "Small Town Growth in the United States: An Analysis by Size, Class, and by Place." *Demography* 3 (1966): 513–27.

Gale, Zona. *Birth.* New York: Macmillan, 1923.

———. *Friendship Village.* New York: Macmillan, 1908.

———. *Friendship Village Love Stories.* New York: Macmillan, 1909.

Gallaher, Art, Jr. *Plainville Fifteen Years Later.* New York: Columbia University Press, 1961.

Givens, Charles. *All Cats Are Gray.* Indianapolis: Bobbs-Merrill, 1937.

Hacker, David W. "Back to the Boonies: Small Towns Thrive as Urban Migration Reverses." *The National Observer,* 5 January 1974, pp. 1–2.

Hart, John F. "Vermontville and Augusta: A Study of Two Michigan Villiages." *Papers, Michigan Academy of Science, Arts, and Letters* 49 (1964): 413–21.

Hatch, Elvin. *Biography of a Small Town.* New York: Columbia University Press, 1979.

Herron, Ima. *The Small Town in American Literature.* New York: Pageant, 1959.

Hicks, Granville. *Small Town.* New York: Macmillan, 1946.

Hilfer, Anthony C. *The Revolt from the Village, 1915–1930.* Chapel Hill: University of North Carolina Press, 1969.

Hilton, George, and Due, John F. *The Electric Interurban Railways In America.* Palo Alto, Calif.: Stanford University Press, 1960.

Hoffer, C. P. *Changes in the Retail and Service Facilities of Rural Trade Centers in Michigan, 1900–1930.* Bulletin 261. East Lansing: Michigan Agricultural Experiment Station, 1935.

Hollingshead, August B. *Elmtown's Youth: The Impact of Social Classes on Adolescents.* New York: Wiley, 1949.

Horgan, Paul. *Whitewater.* New York: Farrar, Straus, and Giroux, 1969.

Houston, Noel. *The Great Promise.* New York: Reynal and Hitchcock, 1946.

Howe, Edgar W. *Story of a Country Town.* Boston: Houghton Mifflin, 1927.

Hughes, Langston. *Not Without Laughter.* New York: Knopf, 1930.

Hunt, Tim. *Kerouac's Crooked Road: Development of a Fiction.* Hamden, Conn.: Archon, 1981.

Jackson, J. B. "The Almost Perfect Town." *Landscape* 2 (spring 1952): 2–8.

———. *American Space.* New York: Norton, 1972.

———. "Metamorphosis." *Annals, Association of Amercian Geographers* 62 (June 1972): 155–58.

———. "Notes and Comments." *Landscape* 17 (autumn 1967): 1–4.

———. "The Stranger's Path." *Landscape* 7 (autumn 1957): 11–15.

Jewett, Sarah Orne. *The Country of the Pointed Firs.* New York: Anchor, 1956.

Kerouac, Jack. *On The Road.* New York: Viking, 1955.

Kerr, Elizabeth M. *Yoknapatawpha: Faulkner's "Little Postage Stamp of Native Soil".* New York: Fordam University Press, 1969.

King, Mary. *Quince Bolliver.* New York: Grosset and Dunlap, 1923.

Knapp, R. H., and Goodrich, H. B. *Origins of American Scientists.* Chicago University of Chicago Press, 1952.

Kolb, J. H. and Brunner, Edmund de S. *A Study of Rural Society: Its Organization and Changes.* Boston: Houghton Mifflin, 1935.

Kolb, J. H., and Day, Leroy J. *Interdependence in Town and Country Relations in Rural Society.* Research Bulletin 172. Madison: Wisconsin Agricultural Experiment Station, 1950.

Lane, Rose Wilder. *Old Home Town.* New York: Longmans, Green,

1935.

Lavender, David. "A Rocky Mountain Fantasy: Telluride, Colorado." In *A Vanishing America: The Life and Times of the Small Town,* Edited by Thomas C. Wheeler. New York: Holt, Rinehart, and Winston, 1964.

Lee, E. S., et al. *An Introduction To Urban Decentralization Research.* Springdale, Va.: National Technical Information Source, U.S. Department of Commerce, 1971.

Lewis, Peirce. "Small Town in Pennsylvania." *Annals, Association of American Geographers* 62 (June 1972): 323–73.

Lewis, Sinclair. *Main Street.* (New York: New American Library, 1961).

Lingeman, Richard. *Small Town America: A Narrative History 1620–The Present.* New York: G. P. Putman's Sons, 1980.

Lockridge, Ross. *Raintree County.* Boston: Houghton Mifflin, 1947.

Lyford, Joseph. *The Talk of Vandalia.* New York: Harper, 1964.

Maddox, Jerald C., ed. *Walker Evans: Photographer for the Farm Security Administration 1935–1938.* New York: Da Capo, 1975.

Marshall, D. G. "Hamlets and Villages in The American Way of Life." *American Sociological Review* 11 (April 1946): 159–65.

Martindale, Don, and Hanson, R. Galen. *Small Town and the Nation: The Conflict of Local and Translocal Forces.* Westport, Conn.: Greenwood, 1969.

Mason, Gregory. "Chatauqua: Its Technic." *The American Mercury* 1 (February 1924): 274–80.

Masters, Edgar Lee. *Spoon River Anthology.* New York: Crowell, 1916.

Mayo, Selz C. "Small Town, U.S.A." *Country Life Association Proceedings* 41 (July 1962): 74–87.

Meinig, D. W. "Symbolic Landscapes: Models of American Community." In *The Interpretation of Ordinary Landscapes,* Edited by D. W. Meinig. New York: Oxford University Press, 1979.

[Mencken, H. L.] "Are Small Towns Doomed?" *The American Mercury* 32 (May 1934): 75.

Michener, James. *Centennial.* New York: Random House, 1974.

Miller, Elva. *Town and Country.* Chapel Hill: University of North Carolina Press, 1928.

Moline, Normal T. *Mobility and the Small Town, 1900–1930.* Research Paper no. 132. Chicago: University of Chicago, Department of Geography, 1971.

Moore, Gary T., and Golledge, Reginald G., eds. *Environmental Knowing.* Stroudsburg, Pa.: Dowden, Hutchinson, and Ross, 1976.

Morris, Wright. *The Home Place.* New York: Scribner's, 1948.

Morrison, Paul C. "A Morphological Study of Worthington, Ohio." *Ohio Journal of Science* 34 (January 1934): 31–45.

Nelson, Lowry. *The Minnesota Community: Country and Town in Transition.* Minneapolis: University of Minnesota Press, 1960.

Nicholson, Meredith. *A Hoosier Chronicle.* Boston: Houghton Mifflin, 1912.

O'Connor, Richard. *Sinclair Lewis.* New York: McGraw-Hill, 1971.

Odell, Clarence B. "The Functional Pattern of Villages in a Selected Area of the Corn Belt." Ph.D. dissertation, University of Chicago, 1937.

O'Hara, John. *Appointment in Samarra.* New York: Harcourt, Brace, 1934.

Paulsen, Arnold, and Carlson, Jerry. "Is Rural Main Street Disappearing?" *Better Farming Methods* 33 (December 1961): 12–14.

Porteous, J. Douglas. *Environment and Behavior.* Reading, Mass.: Addison-Wesley, 1977.

Poston, Richard W. *Small Town Renaissance.* New York: Harper, 1950.

Price, Edward T., Jr. "The Central Courthouse Square in the American County Seat." *Geographical Review* 58 (1968): 29–60.

Redfield, Robert. *The Little Community.* Chicago: University of Chicago Press, 1955.

Reid, Loren. *Hurry Home Wednesday: Growing up in a Small Missouri Town, 1905–1921.* Columbia: University of Missouri Press, 1978.

Relph, E. *Place and Placelessness.* London: Pion, 1976.

Reyher, Ferdinand. *I Heard Them Sing.* Boston: Little, Brown, 1946.

Richter, Conrad. "Individualists Under the Shade Trees; Pine Grove, Pennsylvania." In *A Vanishing America: The Life and Times of the Small Town,* edited by Thomas C. Wheeler. New York: Holt, Rinehart, and Winston, 1964.

Rifkind, Carole. *Main Street: The Face of Urban America.* New York: Harper and Row, 1971.

Riley, Robert. "New Mexico Villages in a Future Landscape." *Landscape* 18 (winter 1969): 3–12.

Roberts, Dorothy James. *A Man of Malice Landing.* New York: Macmillan, 1943.

Sims, Newell L. *A Hoosier Village.* New York: Columbia University Press, 1912.

Sinclair, Harold. *Years of Illusion.* Garden City, N.Y.: Doubleday, Doran, 1941.

Smith, Page. *As a City Upon a Hill: The Town in American History.* New York: Knopf, 1966.

Smith, Suzanne M. *An Annotated Bibliography of Small Town Research.* Madison: University of Wisconsin, Department of Rural Sociology, 1970.

Smith, T. Lynn. "The Role of the Village in American Rural Society." *Rural Sociology* 7 (1942): 10–21.

Stafford, Howard A., Jr. "The Functional Bases of Small Towns." *Economic Geography* 39 (April 1963): 165–75.

Stegner, Wallace. *Second Growth.* Boston: Houghton Mifflin, 1947.

Stewart, George R. *U.S. 40: Cross Section of the United States.* Boston: Houghton Mifflin, 1953.

Strong, Philip D. *Iron Mountain.* New York: Farrar, Straus, and Giroux, 1941.

Stryker, Roy Emerson, and Wood, Nancy. *In This Proud Land: America 1935–1943 As Seen in the F.S.A. Photographs.* Boston: New York Graphic Society, 1973.

Swanson, Bert E., and Cohen, Richard A. *The Small Town in America: A Guide For Study and Community Development.* Rensselaerville, N.Y.: Institute on Man and Science, 1976.

Sweet, Fred Oney. "An Iowa County Seat." *Iowa Journal of History and Politics* 38 (October 1940): 339–408.

Tarkington, Booth. *The Conquest of Canaan.* New York: Harper, 1905.

———. *The Gentleman from Indiana.* New York: Doubleday and McClure, 1900.

Van Doren, Carl. "Sinclair Lewis and the Revolt from the Village." In *Twentieth Century Interpretations of Arrowsmith: A Collection of Critical Essays,* edited by Robert J. Griffen. Englewood Cliffs, N.J.: Prentice-Hall, 1968.

Veblen, Thorstein. "The Country Town." *Freeman* 7 (11 July 1923): 417–20 and (18 July 1923): 440–43.

Vidich, Arthur J., and Bensman, Joseph. *Small Town in Mass Society: Class, Power, and Religion in a Rural Community.* Garden City, N.Y.: Anchor, 1960.

Warner, Lloyd, et al. *Democracy in Jonesville: A Study in Quality and Inequality.* New York: Harper, 1949.

Warren, Robert Penn. *The Circus in the Attic: And Other Stories.* New York: Harcourt, Brace, 1931.

Watts, May T. *Reading the Landscape.* New York: Collier, 1975.

West, James. *Plainville U.S.A.* New York: Columbia University Press, 1946.

West, Pamela. "The Rise and Fall of the American Porch." *Landscape* 20 (spring 1976): 42–47.

Wheeler, Thomas C., ed. *A Vanishing America: The Life and Times of The Small Town.* New York: Holt, Rinehart, and Winston, 1964.

White, William Allen. *What People Said.* New York: Viking, 1938.

White, William Allen. *The Autobiography of William Allen White.* New York: Macmillan, 1946.

Wilder, Thornton. *Our Town: A Play in Three Acts.* New York: Coward McCann, 1938.

Wilkins, Mary E. *The Portion of Labor.* New York: Harper, 1901.

Williams, Harold S. "Smallness and the Small Town." *Small Town* 18 (October 1977): 7–15.

Williams, James M. *An American Town.* New York: J. Kempster, 1906.

Wilson, Harold E. "The Roads of Windsor." *Geographical Review* 21 (July 1931): 353– 97.

Woiwode, Larry. *Beyond the Bedroom Wall: A Family Album.* New York: Avon, 1976.

Wolfe, M. R. "Small Town, Puget Sound Region." *Landscape* 9 (winter 1959–60): 10–13.

Zelinsky, Wilbur. "The Pennsylvania Town: An Overdue Geographical Account." *Geographical Review* 67 (April 1977): 127–47.

INDEX